Treason doth never prosper.
What's the reason?
For if it prosper none dare call it treason.

Sir John Harington, 1561-1612

TREASON AT MAASTRICHT

The destruction of the Nation State

Rodney Atkinson   Norris McWhirter CBE

with contributions by Daniel Hannan

Published by
Compuprint Publishing
1 Sands Road
Swalwell
Newcastle-upon-Tyne
NE16 3DJ

First edition 1994
Second revised and expanded edition 1995

Paperback £5.95 ISBN 0 9509353 9 5
Hardback £11.95 ISBN 0 9525110 1 0

Printed by C.P. Print Limited
Newcastle-upon-Tyne

British Library Cataloguing in Publication Data.
A Catalogue record for this book is available from the
British Library

COMMENTS ON THIS BOOK

"I have read it right through. I agree with the points made and have bought more copies to circulate here among other judges."

A High Court Judge

Refering to the oath of British Privy Counsellors who swear to serve the European Union:

"I cannot reconcile the conflict. I feel that they should resolve the conflict by deciding to bear allegiance to one or other, and not to both sovereigns."

Privy Counsellor and former Lord of Appeal in Ordinary

"Having read it carefully I can only say that it is a masterly work, truly inspirational."

"The book is superb."

ACKNOWLEDGMENT
The authors wish to express their thanks for all his help with the treason cases to Peter Johnston who was one of the first to "dare call it treason".

Cartoon by Richard Willson

CONTENTS

Preface to the Second Edition   1

Introduction   7

1. Europe, Allegiance and and the Bilderbergers   11
2. The Threat to British and American Sovereignty   24
3. Treasonable Aspects of the Maastricht Treaty   34
4. The Treason Cases   43
5. Reply to the Crown Prosecution Service   52
6. Maastricht and UK General Elections   54
7. Lady Thatcher and Lord Tonypandy - speeches   57
   in the House of Lords.
8. Churchill, Europe and the "British Family of Nations"   65
9. Open letter to the 445 Peers who voted against the   69
   Maastricht referendum amendment
10. The EC's growing control of taxation   72
11. Maastricht Treaty invalid   75
12. Government a judge in its own cause   79
13. European superstate backed by Tories   82
14. European Parliament plan to end the nation state   86
15. Federalism and Conservative MEPs   88
16. The European Parliament: a negation of democracy   97
17. American Federalism and European Nations   107
18. The Nazi origins of the European Union   118
19. The new Euro-fascists in Brussels and London   126
20. The Threat from Germany Today   132
21. Chronology of the passage of the Maastricht Bill   143
22. Roll of Honour - Members of the House of Lords   146
    voting for a referendum on Maastricht

Conclusion   149

AppendixI Further notes on the Bilderbergers   154

Appendix II Costs of a Euro-MP   155

The Authors   156

Index   157

CONTENTS

Preface to the Second Edition

Introduction

1. Europe, Maastricht and the Bundesbank

2. The Threat to British and American Sovereignty

3. The Disputable Aspect of the Maastricht Treaty

4. The Treason Cases

5. Reply to the Crown Prosecution Service

6. Maastricht and UK General Election

7. Roy Jenkins and Lord Tonypandy – speeches in the House of Lords

8. Churchill, Europe and the "British Family of Nations"

9. Legal reasons: the 415 Peers who voted against the Maastricht referendum amendment

10. The EC's growing control of national...

11. Maastricht Treaty invalid

12. Government a judge in its own cause

13. European apparatus backed by force

14. European Parliament's part to end the nation state

15. Federalist and Conservative MEPs

16. The European Parliament: a machine of federalism

17. American Federalism and European Union

18. The Flag of tyranny of the European Union

19. The new Euro-fascism in Brussels and Europe

20. The Threat from Germany/Italy

21. Chronology of the passage of the Maastricht Bill

22. Roll of Honour: Members of the House of Lords voting for a referendum on Maastricht

Conclusion

Appendix I Further notes on the Bilderbergers

Appendix II Close of a Europe...

The Authors

Index

PREFACE TO THE
SECOND EDITION

A second edition of this book has become necessary six months after the launch of the first for the best of reasons - that demand has outstripped supply - and for the worst of reasons - that the destruction of the British constitution in particular and the nation state in general continues apace.

The second edition contains 5 new chapters; on Allegiance, Europe and the conspiracy of the "Bilderbergers"; on Churchill, Europe and the British family of nations; on American federalism and European nations; on the threat from Germany today; and on the international attacks on both British and American Sovereignty.

This edition puts the destruction of the British constitution in the context of long running attempts by certain international "cabals" to destroy nation states, first in the pursuit of trade blocks and supranational empire building and secondly in the wider, more secret, agenda to establish world government.

In this process 3 different groups of journalists/politicians/businessmen can be defined: the gullible and weak, so easily enticed by promises of preferment or bullied by threat of expulsion (a group which has grown in number with the rise of the highly dependent professional politician); the opportunists, who will sell any principle, any democratic institution and even their country for the sake of putative commercial gain; and finally, and most pernicious, the treasonous ideologues (often with a social, political or cultural grudge against their country) who have conspired for many decades to destroy national self government and replace it with supranational control by an unaccountable concoction of businessmen, politicians and bureaucrats.

What all three groups have in common is a contempt for democracy and the nations they claim, in public, to serve. What is so fantastic about the ineptitude of British political leaders (Conservative, Labour and Liberal) in their abject surrender of national self government, is their genuine belief (and nothing is more genuine than the beliefs of the truly ignorant) that, even after the legislative surrenders of 1972, 1986 and 1993, no constitutional change has taken place. Blair, Major and Ashdown even today contemplate a referendum only on future, further moves towards a United States of Europe. By such a future referendum of course, those who have already given away the people's democratic rights, hope to sweep under the carpet the constitutional outrages already committed.

The entire British legal system has been subordinated to the European Court - a fact so frustratingly evident to our judges (see comments at the beginning of this book). The British people have had their passports taken away and been turned into "European citizens" with (as yet unspecified) obligations and duties towards the "European Union". Her Majesty the Queen (also now a European Citizen!) has, like Her country, been deprived of Her sovereignty and been put into a position of suzerainty. Her Majesty can now be arraigned in her own courts under the law of another sovereignty. The British Parliament may discuss policies and pass motions but in virtually every area of economic, social, industrial relations, environment, energy, fishing, agriculture, trade, pensions, and employment policy it must defer to "Europe". The laws of the United Kingdom are now made in the form of directives and regulations from Brussels, without having ever been proposed in the election manifesto of a British political party and for the most part not even debated by the Westminster parliament. UK laws can be suspended by the European Court - a "court" which by its own admission is dedicated to promoting

2

European integration. The Court creates new law almost weekly and the British people are powerless to resist.

Eleven other countries were able to take away British fishing rights in internationally recognised territorial waters, and divide them among themselves and they can, by turning anyone in the world into nationals of their own country, thereby create "European Citizens" with the right of entry into (and rights of residence and voting in) the United Kingdom. From 1996 the EU, not the British government, will decide who from non EU countries (ie including the Commonwealth) can or cannot enter the United Kingdom. The Government has caused Her Majesty the Queen to break Her own Coronation Oath whereby she swore for the duration of Her reign, to govern the British people "according to their laws". Even the government has admitted (see chapter 6) that the European Court, not the British people, now makes our laws.

After this litany of incompetence and betrayal, British politicians have the unmitigated gall to deny there is any issue which they must refer to the British electorate. Douglas Hurd, who has spent his entire working life in the diplomatic and foreign service still has not understood the meaning of the most basic terms of government. In The Times of the 3rd January 1995 Hurd is quoted as contrasting his opposition to European "federalism" with his support for "decentralisation". The two terms are not opposites. It is possible to have a highly centralised federalism like the United Kingdom or a decentralised federalism like Germany but in both cases it is quite clear that the ultimate authority and sovereignty rest, respectively, with the British and German governments. A "decentralised" European government is still a European government (with all the trappings and power of a state) and not a British government, controlled by the sovereign British people. That Her Majesty's Secretary of State for Foreign and Commonwealth Affairs has not grasped this elementary truth is truly incredible.

3

It was of course that same Secretary of State who made clear to the British House of Commons that if the Danes said "No" at a second referendum then Britain would abandon the European Union legislation. Then, at the last moment while in Denmark on the eve of that referendum, he said precisely the opposite, leaving the Danish "No" campaign in the lurch. If Quisling had a special meaning for the Norwegians, Hurd has a special meaning for the Danes.

That same Secretary of State recently said in an interview that "the German ratification (of the Maastricht Treaty) was a bit iffy". In the first edition of this book (with the help of the Governor of the Bank of England and his equivalent in Denmark) we proved that the German Court had not in fact ratified the treaty as signed (see chapter 11). Ratification either took place or it was "a bit iffy" but, like virginity, there is no intermediate state. In fact the entire treaty falls since Germany did not, as the Treaty requires, "ratify according to its own constitutional requirements". This episode as well as the other embarassing replies given by Ministers to questions initiated by us in the House of Lords (see below) show how disgraceful this entire process has been. Duplicitous, deceitful, obfuscating and ruthless, the "democratic" politicians have betrayed their countries in the name of a "European" strategy created out of sight of their electorates.

It is at least still possible for us to publish this book on acts of treason against the British nation. But unless our fellow citizens wake up to what is happening to them those who campaign to preserve our nationhood and sovereignty may soon be arraignable before the "European Court" for treason against the European Union!

The "Conservative" government recently withdrew the Whip from eight of its own MPs. The last time the Whip was so withdrawn was during World War II when a Tory MP left the country and declared for Hitler. Now the leaders of a Conservative government have repeated the process - against those who today reject the Euro-fascism of Hitler's children.

4

If the British Conservative Party is in crisis, the Labour Party is in an even deeper crisis. The European Union already rules out the traditional policies of a Labour government - trade union closed shop, import controls and state and regional subsidies without the approval of Brussels. In addition the Labour Party, while proposing further devolution of power to Wales and Scotland, and encouraging Brussels to go straight to the regions, bypassing Westminster, threatens to drive both (predominantly socialist) countries out of the United Kingdom and to destroy for ever the prospect of a Labour government in London (however subsidiary to the European Community). Labour propose a referendum on how the British people vote but refused a Euro-referendum on whether the British people govern themselves at all. The Labour Party believes in certain social and employment rights and subsidies but instead of legislating themselves at Westminster they wish the "Social Chapter" of the Maastricht Treaty to take away from British politicians for all time the right to make such policies. They are prepared to allow European communists and fascists to impose their social policies on the British people.

One million two hundred thousand British people died in two world wars this century, defending the right to nationhood, monarchy, democracy, the rule of law, self government, parliamentary sovereignty and the right to decide who can enter and reside in our country. They also died that national self government be returned to the nations of Europe which Germany had twice sought to destroy. Each year on Remembrance Sunday we remember those who were killed. At remembrance services the national anthem is sung with the words, (refering to the Queen) "may she defend our laws". But today we do not make our laws and "the Queen in parliament" cannot defend them. Those 1.2 million may well have died in vain if the British people do not sweep from office those who have betrayed them and who show every sign of continuing that betrayal.

One of the most frightening aspects of the Clinton-Kohl-Mitterand conspiracy for a "United States of Europe" is the way the West has reacted to the Chechnya crisis. Here we have a blatant case of imperial conquest and repression, the desire of a nation to be free and sovereign and a brutal central power "preserving the union" by destroying the capital and killing the people of that nation. Moscow and the "democratic West" were undoubtedly hoping to brush this scandal under the carpet as the Russian army achieved a swift military victory out of sight of television cameras. Moscow declared that "the West will understand the situation" and the great leaders of the democracies, bent on their own versions of a union from which there is no secession, have remained shamefully silent. How inconvenient that the Chechnyan nation is so resilient.

This second edition is, we believe, a fuller and more forceful reminder than the first, of the two opposing world philosophies which are today engaged in a great struggle for supremacy. On the one hand, the liberal, individualist, nationist, free trading world associated with the Anglo-Saxon economies and their well established democratic parliaments. On the other, the state dominated, collectivist, protectionist, integrationist superpower world of would-be federal empires, too ashamed of their anti-democratic past to wish to defend their discredited nations. There is no doubt that if this latter group triumphs in Europe, the same dark forces which arose in the 1930s will threaten the world again. This book is our modest but heartfelt contribution to the battle.

INTRODUCTION
Rodney Atkinson

Without our Democracy we can justify nothing
Without our Parliament we can do nothing
Without our country we are nothing

The passage of the European Communities (Amendments) Act in 1993 was but the latest in a series of constitutional outrages perpetrated by the British Government on those who elect them. Ever since Edward Heath lied to the electorate about the retention of national sovereignty when Parliament considered the European Communities Act in 1972, the process whereby the British people and Parliament have been deceived, seduced, cajoled and threatened into the European Superstate is unparalleled in democratic history.

The naked aggression of that other builder of "Europe" in the 20th century, Adolf Hitler, was overt and - eventually thanks to men of intelligence like Churchill - understood by the British people. Since 1972, in a slow, secretive but inexorable process, aggression has been replaced by guile, bombs by "Community" directives, armed forces by Brussels bureaucrats and the killing of civilians by the suspension of their laws and the emasculation of their Parliament.

Not long ago I was pleased to spend time chatting with the then German ambassador to the United Kingdom, Baron von Richthofen, a most intelligent and civilised man, related, albeit distantly, to the first world war flying ace of that name. The first time we met we talked of my 6 years working in Germany and our mutual admiration for each other's country.

7

He particularly admired British industry, which he said at its best was far superior to Germany's, British diplomacy and the open and democratic nature of our politics. On the second occasion, the Maastricht debate was in full swing and our conversation was less harmonious. He said that "Germany must be politically integrated into the European Community because we have so many politically dangerous elements in Germany".

Here in a nutshell we have the driving force behind the juggernaut of the European Superstate. Whereas in the 1930's it was Germany's strength and aggression which attempted to create a united Europe (and which was even called a "European Economic Community", see below, Chapter 14) today it is Germany's fear of its own political weakness. There can be no more dangerous foundation for any venture than the fear of its alternative.

Needless to say I expressed my concern to the ambassador that if Germany had such dangerous and destabilising problems then they must be resolved in Germany by Germans. Those who cannot solve their own problems make dangerous partners for others.

It is not surprising that when in peacetime men pursue the destruction of nations and the takeover of Parliamentary sovereignty (which would otherwise be the aims of war), then extraordinary violence must be done to the legal and constitutional structures of democratic countries. This is nowhere more true than in the use of the Crown Prerogative by the British Government to sign the Maastricht Treaty. The subsequent passage of the European Communities (Amendment) Act had nothing to do with the approval of the Treaty for which the Government (and the Crown Prosecution Service in their refutation of our court cases) called exclusively on their treaty making powers under the Crown Prerogative.

The Prerogative is the power of Her Majesty's Government to act without the authority of Parliament. It is assumed (dangerously as Maastricht proved) that the Government of the day will automatically act in the interests of the country as a whole in its international relations, in matters of national emergency and in a number of other responsibilities.

But it is quite clear that, like the Treaty of Rome, the Maastricht Treaty is not just an agreement between nations about international conduct but rather it is a **constitutional** agreement which seriously affects the **internal** activities of a nation state, the democratic rights of the people and the legal authority of the courts.

No international agreement which permits those countries to determine who has the right to enter, reside in and vote in Britain, which permits an alien authority to lay down minimum tax rates and impose and suspend laws without reference to the British Parliament, could possibly be described as covering the issues normally associated with inter-nation treaty making.

The British people approved, by voting, only one kind of association with that narrow group of countries which constitute less than a third of the countries of Europe - an association of free trading sovereign nations, with cooperation on legal and regulatory matters only in so far as it is necessary in the pursuit of that free trade. A "Common Market" expressed that notion. But a Single Market, which resulted from the 1986 legislation (even less understood or discussed than the Maastricht Treaty) is a world away from a common market. Indeed a single market is a contradiction in terms - just as the traditional French and German notions of protectionism, mercantilism and state intervention are alien to the notions of individualism and international trade which have been the basis of anglo-saxon political economy.

Individualism and liberal trade policies are the foundation of the nation state and even democracy itself. Despite the evident gulf between the British people and their Parliamentary representatives on the "European" issue there has at least been a long drawn out debate, heated controversy and a measure of analysis not seen anywhere else in Europe. In Portugal the entire Treaty passed through Parliament in less than an hour. In Germany three quarters of the Parliament agreed to give up the Deutschmark and approve the Treaty while 85% of Germans disapproved of the former and 70% opposed the latter. In both Denmark and France half the population opposed the Treaty. In Ireland the Government lied to the electorate.

We took Government Ministers to Court in the UK on eight counts of treason and destruction of the Constitution because at no stage were either the British people nor the British Courts called upon to examine the constitutionality of the whole Treaty (despite the Rees Mogg case). The Treaty itself was not published until after the general election which John Major claimed approved it.

The end results of our treason cases were statements from the Crown Prosecution Service in England and the Lord Advocate in Scotland. While declining to address the specific charges at all the Government's prosecution services in both countries claimed that the only justification required was the passage of the European Communities (Amendments) Act 1993 and that if there were any conflicts with case law or statutes in force then that Act removed them by over-riding eight hundred years of Parliamentary law. If there were treason then it was perfectly legal treason. If the constitution had been destroyed then our flexible constitution permitted its own destruction.

We firmly believe that this scandalous situation is not, nor ever will be, approved by the British people. We hope that this modest publication describing our efforts to restore the British Constitution will serve as an historical record of these tragic events.

1.

EUROPE, ALLEGIANCE AND THE BILDERBERGERS

"For everyone that does evil hates the light."
John 3: 19

The concept of allegiance dates, in Britain, back to the 14th century. King Henry IV was styled my 'liege lord'. His subjects were termed 'liege subjects' and were bound to serve and obey him. The present day definition of allegiance is: (Halsbury's Laws of England)

> "...the tie or obligation of a subject to his sovereign or government."

Halsbury further asserts:

> 'The essence of the offence of treason lies in the violation of the allegiance owed to the Sovereign. Allegiance is due from all British subjects wherever they may be.'

The two leading cases on the natural duty of allegiance are R v Casement, 1916 and Joyce v Director of Public Prosecutions, 1946. Sir Roger Casement CMG (1864-1916) had been author of two immensely valuable Foreign Office reports on Belgian atrocities in the Congo rubber plantations (1903) and on atrocities in Peruvian plantations in 1912. However in 1914 he worked to gain German aid to win complete Irish independence and travelled to Berlin in November of that year. On his return, after landing from a U-Boat near Tralee, he was arrested by police on 24th April, 1916, tried at the Old Bailey

(26-29 June), convicted of treason and sentenced to death. His knighthood was annulled, his appeal failed and he was hanged at Pentonville Prison, London, on 3rd August. The American-born William Joyce (1906-1946), after being expelled from Sir Oswald Moseley's British Union of Fascists in 1937, formed his own fanatically pro-Hitler British National Socialist Party. Having fled to Germany he became a propaganda broadcaster with a drawling, pretentious accent, for Radio Hamburg, from September 1939 until April 1945. The British Passport for which he had applied had been valid until July 1940. He too was tried at the Old Bailey, convicted, sentenced and hanged at Wandsworth prison on 3rd January, 1946.

(Now that the new European Community passport is replacing the traditional British passport, one of the evidential linchpins of treason is being deliberately or inadvertently surrendered.)

It should not be thought that the duty of the subject to the sovereign is one-sided. The very descent of the Crown by a monarch since 1688 has been subject to the taking of a Coronation oath in a statutorily provided form. Under the Coronation Oath Act 1953 the Queen undertook the duty:

> 'to govern the peoples of the United Kingdom of Great Britain and Northern Ireland (and the dominions overseas etc.) according to their respective laws and customs.'

The concept of the laws belonging to the people is encapsulated in s.4 of the Act of Settlement, 1700 wherein it is declared that 'the laws of England are the birthright of the people thereof and all the kings and queens who shall ascend the throne of this realm ought to serve them respectively according to the same......'. It is noted, of course, that in its legal sense the word 'ought' is a mandatory 'must'.

It has been established in law since the time of the first Elizabeth, per Nichols v Nichols, 1576, that the royal prerogative is created for the benefit of the people and cannot be exerted to their prejudice'.

On or about 17th January, 1972, the Foreign and Commonwealth Office applied for full powers under royal prerogative to enable Mr. (now Sir Edward) Heath, Sir Alec Douglas-Home (now Lord Home) and Mr. Geoffrey Rippon (now Lord Rippon of Hexham), to go to Brussels as plenipotentiaries to sign, on behalf of the United Kingdom, a Treaty of Accession to the unamended Treaty of Rome, which had been operated by West Germany, France, Italy, The Netherlands, Belgium and Luxembourg since 1956.

On being requested for these treaty-making prerogative powers on the advice, indeed the insistence of her elected government, the Queen, as a constitutional monarch, granted them. In law, while the Queen could do no wrong, she can be deceived in her grant and in this case plainly was. Accession was the death knell of the monarchy itself.

So began the stealthy step-by-step, ratchet-like process, which put the Queen in breach of her own solemn, legally-binding, Coronation Oath, an oath which applies not for part of her reign but for the whole of it. It was, of course, the start of a process which not merely undermined, but destroyed allegiance to the Crown insofar as the monarch was diminished, demeaned and downgraded to the status of a European citizen co-equal with the status of her unconsulted and bemused subjects.

The only relevant and permissible description for conduct of this kind is the adjective 'treasonous'. The treason which culminated in Maastricht had begun in Brussels nearly 20 years earlier. The 1972 European Communities Act contained the original 'time bombs' which destroyed the British constitution but the timing of their explosion was - deliberately - delayed. Detonation did not occur until many directives and regulations from Brussels and (most perniciously) the judgements of the European court applied that 1972 enactment to ever more policy areas. Needless to say no British minister or British parliament could, by then, challenge or change such directives or judgements.

In English law it has been held that the treaty-making power, being an exercise of royal prerogative, cannot be impugned in the courts (McWhirter v Attorney General, 1972). On 30th June, 1972 the Court of Appeal (the Master of the Rolls, Lord Denning; Lords Justices Phillimore and Cairns) were sitting at a time between the decision in principle in parliament (of which they could take no judicial cognizance) and the intended enactment of the European Communities Act, containing the notorious and ingenious Section 2. The court did not fully address itself to the argument that, for obvious reasons, the royal prerogative may not be exercised in any way that is innovatory. If the law permitted any government at will to extend the use of the royal prerogative into new fields, the legislative role of parliament could be bypassed. Embarrassingly, the Command Paper 3301 (1967) entitled *Legal and Constitutional Implications of the United Kingdom's Membership of the European Community* had already officially confirmed that constitutionally the then putative membership of the EEC would indeed be "without precedent", ie. the prerogative used to sign the Treaty of Accession would be indeed a novel and therefore impermissible extension of the power.

While the Court of Appeal predictably ruled that this summons, unreported in any English Law Reports, 'disclosed no reasonable cause of action', the judges did not explain how, if treaty- making was within the amplitude of the prerogative power, the limitation on innovation did not, in some curious way, apply in the field of the making of treaties. We are thus left with the juridical nonsense of an unfettered part of a fettered whole. When the day comes, as assuredly it will, that some future United Kingdom government desires or is driven to decide to withdraw from a federal European Union, the initiative behind this case may prove to be of great value. Meanwhile the Court of Justice of the European Communities insists that its ruling in Costa v E. N. E. L., 1964, makes the withdrawal of a member state impermissible under European law.

14

The Court ruled:

> "The transfer by the states from their domestic legal systems to the Community legal system of the rights and obligations arising under the Treaty carries with it a permanent limitation of their sovereign rights, against which a subsequent unilateral act, incompatible with the concept of the Community cannot prevail."

If however it can be shown that Britain's accession was not 'in accordance with their (her) respective constitutional requirements', then the deposit of the instruments of ratification by Britain in August 1993, must of itself be in breach of Article R of the Treaty. It is our contention that the Treaty of European Union, signed at Maastricht, is in any case invalid since (chapter 11) the Federal German Constitutional Court in Karlsruhe did not approve the treaty as signed.

The genesis of the idea of a United Europe, in which the sovereign nation state is replaced by a federal union of former such states, can be traced further back than the activities of the Frenchman Jean Monnet (1888-1979), who was President of both the European Coal and Steel High Authority (1952-55) and the Action Committee for the United States of Europe (1956).

As early as 1924 the Polish-born Joseph Hieronim Retinger (1888-1960), who had settled in London in 1911, conceived, for reasons of his own, the idea of a united Europe. At various times he was rumoured to have been an agent of bodies as various as the Socialist Internationale, the Freemasons, the Vatican and the government of Mexico. Retinger was a compulsive intriguer and a behind-the-scenes political wheeler-dealer. Others saw him as a penniless adventurer and an irresponsible meddler. Retinger teamed up with a French-born journalist and Labour MP, Georges Edmond Pierre Achille Morel de Ville (1873-1924), later known as Edmund Dene Morel. Morel had worked with Casement (see above) in the Congo Reform Association. He was bellicose, vain and given to self-deception. Morel launched the Union of

Democratic Control (UDC) in 1914 which called for a negotiated peace with Germany. He was later imprisoned for six months for a breach of the Defence of the Realm Act. In 1922 Morel stood for the Labour Party in Dundee against Winston Churchill and won. Such are the vagaries of politics that Morel was seriously considered for the Foreign Secretaryship in the first Labour Government and was also nominated for the Nobel Peace Prize. He became an embittered critic of Labour's first Prime Minister, Ramsay MacDonald, who, with eight other new Cabinet Ministers, had been a UDC colleague of Morel. Morel however soon suffered a heart attack and died in November 1924.

Dr. Retinger had now to look for a new parliamentary ally. He was rebuffed by the General Secretary of the Transport and General Workers' Union, Ernest Bevin (1881-1951) since he proved to be both a patriot and an Empire loyalist. Next Retinger tried Sir Stafford Cripps (1889-1952) who actually embarked on writing a book advocating European unity. With the Hitler-Stalin partition of Poland and the outbreak of World War II in 1939 and Cripps' extraordinary appointment to be British Ambassador in Moscow in 1940, his manuscript, though nearly completed, has yet to see the light of day.

Retinger could hardly continue with his quest for a United Europe when Nazi Germany's concept of unity was demonstrably imperial. It was the aim of the Third Reich to have Italy and Austria as military allies but the Low Countries, France, Denmark and Norway, would be occupied by the Wehrmacht. Britain, under the rule of the specially selected Gauleiter Six, was to become an agricultural and horticultural larder for the "Herrenvolk".

No sooner had Germany been defeated in World War II than Retinger, who had meanwhile been 'political adviser' to Poland's General Sikorski (1881-1943), was back on his old tack. As early as the first anniversary of VE day on 8th May, 1946, he made his first move to set up The European Movement in London. On 29th March, 1949 he was instrumental in setting up the American Committee on a United Europe (ACUE) with the first Director of the CIA (Central Intelligence Agency), Allen Dulles (1893-1969), as Vice Chairman to William 'Wild Bull' Donovan (1883-1959). Nearly $12 million of US public money was siphoned into the European movement through ACUE. One of the Movement's more curious aims was of allowing West Germany to re-arm.

Having recruited Prince Bernhard of the Netherlands (later discredited in the Lockheed scandal of 1976), the ever restless Retinger flew to Washington D.C. to lobby the Director of the CIA, General Walter Bedell Smith, David Rockefeller, Dean Rusk and others to join in a formal conference of other internationally high-powered invitees at the Hotel de Bilderberg in the little Dutch town of Oosterbeek on 29-31 May, 1954. This was the genesis of the secretive annual Bilderberg Conferences. Almost every political and business élite in the West has attended these covert occasions, for which no agenda, minutes or list of attendees is published and for which media publicity is highly discouraged. The US Ambassador to West Germany, George McGhee, who attended the third Bilderberg Conference at Garmisch-Partenkirchen, is on record as saying:

> "The Treaty of Rome, which brought the Common Market
> into being, was nurtured at Bilderberger meetings."
> (Eringer, Robert: *The Global Manipulators*, Pentacle
> Books, Bristol, England; 1980) **See also Appendix I**

A prominent member of the Bilderberg group is Lord Carrington who, as Foreign Secretary, presided over the loss of the Falkland Islands in 1982. It was one of Carrington's officials who boasted to Peter Jay, the former British Ambassador to Washington, that he was on a mission "to ask the Argentinians to take the Falkland Islands".

A recent (22-25 April 1993) Bilderberg conference in Vouliagmeni in Greece was attended by British Chancellor of the Exchequer Kenneth Clarke and by Tony Blair, at that time Shadow Home Secretary and since 1994 leader of the Labour

Party. Many will wish to know how those who owe their positions to national electorates should attend (no doubt at party or public expense) meetings to pursue a secret agenda which (as we have seen in the 'European Union') can have catastrophic consequences for their own unconsulted and uninformed national electorates.

Who are the Bilderbergers?
The following were among those attending the April 1993 Bilderberg conference in Greece:

From the United Kingdom:
Kenneth Clarke, Chancellor of the Exchequer
Tony Blair, (then) Shadow Home Secretary
Eric Roll, President, Warburg Group
Marlin Taylor, Chief Executive, Courtaulds Textiles
Sir Patrick Sheehy, Chairman, BAT Industries
Lord Carrington, Chairman, Christies
Barbara Amiel, Columnist, *Sunday Times*
Conrad Black (husband of Amiel) Chairman, *The Telegraph*
Rodric Braithwaite, Foreign Policy Adviser to John Major
Andrew Knight, Chairman, News International

From the USA:
Paul Allaire Chairman, Xerox Corporation
George Ball, Former US Under Secretary of State
Kenneth Dam, Professor, University of Chicago,
former US Deputy Secretary of State
Stephen Friedman, Chairman, Goldman Sachs
John Galvin, Professor, West Point and former Supreme Allied
Commander SHAPE
James Hoagland, Foreign Correspondent, *Washington Post*
Lane Kirkland, President, AFL-CIO (American equivalent of
British Trade Union Congress)
Samuel Lewis, Director Policy Planning Staff,
US Department of State
William Odom, former Director National Security Agency
Larry Pressler, Senator, South Dakota
David Rockefeller, Chairman, Chase Manhattan

Lyn Williams, International President, United Steel Workers
of America

From Germany:
Volker Rühe Minister of Defence
Theo Sommer, Editor, *Die Zeit*
Lothar Späth, Chief Executive, Jenoptik,
former Prime Minister of Baden Württemberg
Wolfgang Reitzle, Board member BMW
Christoph Bertram, Diplomatic Correspondent, *Die Zeit*
Ulrich Cartellieri, Board member Deutsche Bank

From Denmark:
Uffe Ellemann-Jensen, former Foreign Minister

From France:
Patrick Divedjian, Member of Parliament
Thierry de Montbrial, Director French Institute of
International Relations
Louis Schweitzer, Chairman, Renault

From Greece:
Michalis Papaconstantinou, Minister for Foreign Affairs
Theodore Papalexopoulos, Deputy Chairman, Titan Cement
Thanos Veremis, Professor of Political History, University
of Athens
Themistocles Vokos, Chairman, The Seatrade Organisation
John Lyras, Vice Chairman, Union of Greek Shipowners
Stefanos Manos, Minister of National Economy
Yanis Costopoulos, Chairman, Credit Bank
Stelios Argyros, Chairman, Federation of Greek Industries

From The Netherlands:
Viktor Halberstadt, Professor, Leiden University
(and Bilderberg Honorary Secretary General for Europe!)
Ernst van der Beugel, Emeritus Professor, Leiden (and
former Bilderberg Honorary Secretary General for Europe)
Elco Brinkman, Parliamentary leader of Christian Democrats
Floris Maljers, Chairman, Unilever NV
Wim Kok, Minister of Finance, Deputy Prime Minister

From Ireland:
Peter Sutherland, Chairman, Allied Irish Banks plc,
Former European Commissioner
Conor Brady, Editor, the *Irish Times*

From Austria:
Franz Vranitzky, Federal Chancellor
Peter Jankowitsch, Chairman, Joint Parliamentary Committee
Austria - EC; Former Foreign Minister
Paul Lendvai, Director, Austrian International Radio

From Sweden:
Carl Bildt, Prime Minister
Percy Barnevik, President and Chief Executive,
Asea Brown Boveri

From Italy:
Giovanni Agnelli, Chairman, Fiat

The Bilderbergers have consistently targeted politicians **before** they reach the highest level. Examples include Harold Wilson, Edward Heath, Helmut Schmidt and Tony Blair - and this "talent spotting" seems to be rather more than just a matter of luck. **The Bilderbergers require that combination of corporatism and socialism which so well reflects the philosophy of 1930s fascism.** As Senator Javits declared in the US Congressional record of 11th April 1964 "leading figures are invited who, through their special knowledge and experience, can help to further Bilderberg objectives".

The fascist connection is indeed more personal since the international banker Paul Warburg, a founder of the American (Bilderberg related) "Committee on Foreign Relations" and a proponent of "World Government", was the brother of Max Warburg whose signature appears, along with Hitler's, on the (17.3.1933) appointment of Hjalmar Schacht to the Reichsbank Directorate. The CFR is closely allied with the Royal Institute of International Affairs (Chatham House) in London.

But perhaps the Bilderbergers' greatest coup was the removal from office of Margaret Thatcher in November 1990, which had been planned at a meeting on the island of La Toja off the Atlantic coast of Spain on the weekend of 11th May 1989. The American newspaper *The Spotlight*, published in Washington DC, quoted a source at the meeting, that the Bilderbergers ...

> "emphasised the need to bring down Mrs Thatcher because of her refusal to yield British sovereignty to the European superstate that is to emerge in 1992. Mrs Thatcher was denounced for 'provincialism' and 'nationalism'...Political leaders in Britain who participated were instructed to attack Mrs Thatcher...to force her to yield her nation's sovereignty to save her own government."

Britain's Prime Minister, as we know, said "No, No, No" to the new Eurofascism but within 2 years the Bilderbergers' plan had prevailed. A democratically elected Prime Minister had been dismissed without a general election and an international cabal had conspired to destroy a nation's leader.

The allegiance of Britain's European Commissioners

On 8th December, 1994, letters were sent to the two United Kingdom appointees to the new 1995 European Commission, Sir Leon Brittan and Mr. Neil Kinnock. The letters were identical except in their cross references, and that addressed to Mr. Kinnock is here reproduced. As will be seen, the essence is that working for the European Union undermines the exclusivity inherent in allegiance to the Crown. Before the letters were despatched to Brussels, the advice of two of the country's leading constitutional lawyers was sought. Both agreed that continued membership of the Privy Council (and sworn allegiance to Her Majesty the Queen as Head of State of an independent nation) was wholly incompatible with allegiance to the European Union, with its court, Parliament, passport, flag and even a national anthem.

Breach of oath does not, in English civil law, attract a statutory criminal sanction because it is an offence rather against ecclesiastical law. Ecclesiastical law is, however, part of the law of England and research has been put in hand to discover how such brazen contempt of oath can be brought to public notice in open court.

Commissioner Rt. Hon. Neil Kinnock,
The European Commission,
Brussels 1040, BELGIUM   8th December, 1994

Dear Commissioner Kinnock,

After taking the oath of allegiance and the Privy Counsellor's oath (or an affirmation in lieu of either of those oaths), in 1983 you were called to office as a Privy Counsellor by the sovereign's invitation, and your name was then inscribed in the Council book.

The substance of the oath includes the solemn undertaking

> 'to bear faith and allegiance to the Crown and to defend its jurisdiction and powers against all foreign.....persons.....or states'.

In January however you are required to make a solemn declaration before the Court of Justice of the European Communities:

> 'To perform my duties in complete independence, in the general interest of the Communities'; in carrying out my duties 'neither to seek nor to take instructions from any Government or body; to refrain from any action incompatible with my duties.'

This declaration is intended to be the pledging of a sole allegiance to the European Community. The Commission initiates and implements European Community legislation and is the guardian of the European Community treaties which have inter alia reduced H.M. The Queen, per Article 8 of the Treaty of Union signed at Maastricht, to the status of an ordinary European citizen in common with her subjects and thereby subjected her to duties which are undefined. H.M. The Queen has been rendered by the Treaties, per Article 192 of the Treaty of Rome (as amended and over which HM

22

Government *has failed to provide for any veto*, see Prime Minister's answer to Nigel Spearing MP, 12.4.94), liable to personal taxation in common with all other European citizens. Additionally HM The Queen has been rendered subject to past and future judgments and to arraignments of your Court which is external to the United Kingdom, but which is set in authority over her own Courts in which she was not previously arraignable.

I have taken the opinion of two leading constitutional lawyers to the effect that there is here a clear conflict and that allegiance may be borne "to one or other and not to both sovereigns".

There are many persons, who have been deemed to have become citizens of Europe as from 1st November 1993, who would wish to be enlightened on the dual role of Privy Counsellors who are also Commissioners in Brussels and when or whether Sir Leon Brittan and yourself intend to rectify such a palpable and demoralizing breach of your oaths of allegiance. The jurisdiction of the Crown has been compromised by various judgments of the Court of Justice to which you have declared allegiance whereby United Kingdom statutes in force have been dispensed with or suspended. Furthermore in reply to questions in the House of Lords, H.M. Government has admitted any interpretation of the word 'municipal' in Article 8 of the Treaty of Union (i.e. who could or could not vote in United Kingdom elections) would be for the determination not of H.M. Courts but of the Court of justice of the European Communities - a most fundamental example of a loss of the Crown's jurisdiction which has been undefended.

On appointment to the Commission any consideration of honour, logic and constitutionality would surely indicate that you now must request that your name should be struck from the Council book.

Yours sincerely, NORRIS McWHIRTER

2.

THE THREAT TO BRITISH AND AMERICAN SOVEREIGNTY

GATT, NAFTA AND THE EUROPEAN UNION

The United States and the United Kingdom face the same threats from those conspiring to abolish national sovereignty and replace it with world government. Both Britons and Americans are being inveigled (in the name of free trade between nations) into giving up their rights to nationhood and self government.

Both countries have elements of federalism in their national governance and both face a threat from an external "federal" authority seeking to bypass national government and encourage individual regions and states into a new allegiance with that external authority.

Because both countries have electorates contemptuous of the governments which have proved economically inept the task of the eurofederalists and their cousins in the "world government" movement has been made easier. As usual with the failure of collectivism, its disasters leave fertile ground to argue for more collectivist "solutions".

During the 1980s both countries saw the socialist, collectivist and statist policies which had wrought such destruction in the 1960s and 1970s banished from national politics - although the weak successors to Reagan, and Thatcher (Bush and Major) did much to restore theme. But those elements who had been soundly trounced at the national level (where their failure was well understood and their responsibility to voters clear) gravitated with their failed theories to the supranational level of the United Nations and the "block politics" of Europe and North America. So, just as nations were applying free market principles, supranational organisations were conspiring to integrate nations into "managed" blocks.

We have detailed in this book the destruction of the British Constitution by the Maastricht Treaty and the threat to anglo saxon liberalism (in the classic English sense of the word!) represented by the resurgence of socio-economic fascism in Europe. Here we discuss the threat to American national sovereignty in the North American Free Trade Agreement (NAFTA) and in the latest round of the General Agreement on Tariffs and Trade (GATT). In particular the "World Trade Organisation" the birth of which has been "tacked on" to the GATT has dangerous consequences which have not been grasped either in America or Britain. We will compare these agreements with the treaties of European Union and see how the American government has at least avoided some of the catastrophic mistakes of the British government.

The Comptroller General of the United States begins his report to the US Congress by refering to NAFTA as "a dramatic step in the process of North American economic integration". Despite refering twice on the first page to "liberalising trade and investment in North America" the words "economic integration" are suggestive of a rather less liberal concept.

We have seen how in the European Community a "Common Market" became a covert (and hitherto very successful) attempt at economic, monetary and political integration. Those intent on integration are not renowned for their acceptance of nation states or free international trade. How can "inter-nation" trade take place if nations are integrated into blocks? But it has always been the logic of the collectivist to assume that conflict can only be resolved by the abolition of the conflicting parties.

25

To integrate (Oxford English Dictionary) is to "combine (parts or elements) into a whole". But combining the economies of Canada, Mexico and the USA into one would be as catastrophic as the same process in Europe, not least because the lead in such integration is not taken by free people and competing companies but by politicians and their social interventions.

If NAFTA really were about "liberalising trade and investment" then capital would flow to the areas of its most profitable uses, releasing overpriced labour and investment goods for higher value production and employing lower priced and unutilised labour and goods in poorer areas. Goods and services would flow across borders, enabling labour to remain where it is linguistically and culturally at home. Wealth would be automatically distributed from richer to poorer while simultaneously raising the wealth of all.

But one of the first clauses of the NAFTA is the exclusion of "trade sensitive economic sectors"! "Temporary protection" would be allowed "for industries that are injured by imports" - a definition which gives remarkable scope for extensive application. Mexico made an exception of its oil industry, Canada its "culturally sensitive information industries" and the USA exempted its price and marketing support for agricultural products.

As with the EEC, an ostensible internal market becomes an excuse to tighten controls against those outside thus creating a trade block (and, in response, competing protectionist trade blocks elsewhere in the world). For instance within NAFTA "all barriers to trade in North American automotive goods and all investment restrictions in the automotive sector" will be eliminated within 10 years. But "stringent automotive rules of origin are designed to prevent non NAFTA countries products from enjoying NAFTA's preferential treatment." In other words America is prepared to allow competition for its massive motor industry from countries like Canada and Mexico who represent no threat but not from their true competitors in Europe. Thus has the dangerous logic of the 1930s been rejuvenated in the 1990s. The steps to international disaster are clear: protectionism: trade blocks: trade wars: shooting wars. But this process began not in America but in the European Community whose trade practices are notorious the world over.

For those who have seen the gradual erosion of national sovereignty within the European Community in the name of "free trade" the most ominous elements of the NAFTA process for the USA must be the "parallel negotiations" on environmental protection, workers rights and safety. These are of course precisely the areas in which Britain's sovereign parliament is repeatedly overruled by "Europe", not least as a backdoor method of imposing social legislation despite the British government's opt out from the so called "Social Chapter" of the Maastricht Treaty. The USA should beware - the loss of sovereignty starts with such concepts as "parallel negotiations" or, as at Maastricht, "different pillars".

Just as the first stage of Eurofederalism was the innocuous sounding "European Common Market" with its "Commission" so NAFTA has its "Free Trade Commission" charged not only with implementing the agreement but "addressing unresolved issues" (a dangerously flexible notion!) However, at the instigation of the USA, each country will retain its laws regarding unfair foreign trade practices and may apply these laws (including the notorious American section 301 retaliation) to their NAFTA partners. This is of course a degree of sovereignty which the EC has never allowed - and indeed this kind of sovereign freedom may not survive even in NAFTA.

There is an interesting contrast between the welcome of NAFTA in Mexico, particularly among labour unions (and opposition from American and Canadian unions) while in Europe it is the German government and unions which are pushing hardest for "European integration". This contrast is explained by the "free trade between sovereign nations" espoused by NAFTA and the federalist, interventionist and socialised approach of the European Union. In NAFTA competition for capital between poor Mexican and rich American workers will lead to the enrichment of the former and a challenge to the wages of the latter. NAFTA is expected to produce incremental growth in Canada and America of less than 0.5% of GDP but in Mexico an incremental growth rate of 11%. In Europe the expensive social costs of employing labour in Germany and France are being extended to Greece, Spain and Portugal, ensuring less of a threat to the comfortable incomes of German and French workers and restraining investment from Northern Europe in the poorer economies of southern Europe.

Indeed as this book goes to press the German government is even trying to push through European-wide legislation to stop Portuguese workers working (at excellent rates by their standards) for German companies in Germany. Because the proposed EU directive which would protect German workers and unions from competition has been opposed by Britain, Ireland, Portugal and Greece, Germany is going to legislate unilaterally with even tougher protectionist measures. This is not the first time that Germany, the most fanatical integrationist has exempted itself from the legal structures which apply to its "partners". The German government accepts, indeed promotes, any issue extending political power in Europe while rejecting any measure which represents a challenge to German economic interests (and hence the benefit of other EC member states). Indeed Germany is the second worst implementer of single market legislation.

As the electorates of all "democratic" countries know to their cost, economic change brings temporary dislocation which politicians use as an excuse for permanent state interventions in markets. Unfortunately in both the EC and NAFTA politicians have given themselves golden opportunities to "re-train" and "re-direct" labour. This is of course a recipe for mis-training and misdirection of labour - and at a heavy cost to the very businesses and entrepreneurs who would have efficently re-trained and re-directed labour in the natural course of business!

One of the most dangerous aspects of the processes by which NAFTA, GATT and Maastricht were ratified by the British and American parliaments was the requirement to approve the whole treaty/agreement without amendment. This trend towards overriding national democratic sovereignty by international treaty, in the name of the "new world order" is fascist in concept and practice. The power of international treaty makes redundant national parliaments as power politics overturns or ignores the popular will. Democratic representatives either conspire in this betrayal or meekly accept the "new order". How Hitler, Stalin and Mussolini must regret not living 50 years later in this more friendly environment.

GATT - is America learning the lesson of Maastricht?

Despite the threat to the sovereignty of the United States posed by the new GATT agreement, and in particular the proposed "World Trade Organisation", there are signs from the Bill laid before Congress, that the American government has learned from the disastrous consequences of the Maastricht Treaty for the British constitution.

The Americans are rightly suspicious of a new extension to GATT - a large supranational bureaucracy empowered to administer global trade rules - called the World Trade Organisation (WTO). As we have seen in Europe such organisations start as arbitrators of free trade, applying *existing* rules but soon start creating *new* rules. Then they find that many countries refuse to obey in detail the rules which they agreed in general. The force of a new supranational law is required and a new legal authority is established. (**It is of course never explained why states which reneged on agreements between nations should suddenly start obeying laws within a superstate, to which their citizens have no allegiance.**) In Europe it is precisely those states which are most fanatical integrationists which find themselves most often before the European Court while the most anti-federalist, Britain, is most punctilious in obeying the law. Next, free trade is deemed impossible without the application of the same environmental social, employment and industrial relations laws in all trading countries. The road to "one government" is now all down hill. Before long "federalism" means not decentralisation but an all powerful central authority capable of enforcing obedience on the states or nations who were so foolish as to give birth to such a creature.

After 40 years (and 7 rounds) of the GATT, suddenly in 1994 the free nations of the world were presented with an "add on" WTO. The WTO may of course just be a naive construct of those who want to "solve" international trading conflicts but it is undoubtedly intended by many as an attack on free nations and the first step towards "world government". The WTO turns a free contractual relationship between sovereign nations into an international organisation with powers over nations which no nation can veto. To see the potential effect on world affairs of this "politicisation" we need only look at the enormous tensions in the European Community since 1986 when the Single European Act extended majority voting and since the 1992 Maastricht Treaty when some 11 areas of social, political economic, industrial and environmental decision making became "common European policies", much of which are open to majority voting.

The most disturbing aspect of these collectivist, supranational developments is their contradiction of the very foundations of that open, free trading, contract based international order which has always been promoted and guaranteed by the Anglo Saxon world - and always opposed by fascists and communists in continental Europe and international socialists the world over. Those who replace free contracts with the impositions of majority voting are "collectivists". They should not be confused with those engaged in free collective action, which is spontaneous and confers on those who so act no state or political privilege. Collectivists seek to achieve by political voting and state, or superstate, power the rights, rewards and privileges which their fellow citizens would never grant them in open competition.

Despite these dangers however the US Congress does seem to have avoided the traps into which the Major-Hurd-Clarke led British Government has so disastrously fallen in Europe. Even after 200 years of federal government the GATT legislation makes clear that Washington, following ratification, "must consult with the States for the purpose of achieving conformity of State laws and practices with the Uruguay Round Agreements". Contrast this genuine division of powers and the retention of some semblance of sovereignty in the USA with the terms of the 1972 European Act which give automatic overriding authority to the laws of and treaties signed by the "European Community" over the legal systems of member states.

One of the principal democratic deficiencies of the British constitution is the doctrine of implied repeal, that is a law passed today automatically overrides any previous Act of Parliament or parts thereof which may be in contradiction of it. This occurs without explicitly repealing (and therefore without public discussion of) the statutes thus contradicted. Such a process is a scandalous negation of democracy, even when the laws so extinguished are not basic to the constitution. At Maastricht the constitution of the United Kingdom was decimated covertly with the aid of "implied repeal". The American GATT legislation, by contrast states:

> "No state law or the application of such a state law, may be declared invalid as to any person or circumstance on the ground that the provision or application is inconsistent with any of the Uruguay Round Agreements except in an action brought by the United States for the purpose of declaring such law or application invalid."

The American authorities evidently have a more democratic understanding of fundamental rights enshrined in statutes. The

GATT legislation further makes clear that any judgment of the GATT

> "...Appellate Body concerned under the Dispute Settlement Understanding regarding the state law...shall not be considered as binding or otherwise accorded deference."

This we can contrast with the demands of Hurd and Major in the UK for automatic approval by Parliament of whatever international agreement they have signed under royal prerogative. Moreover in the Maastricht Treaty there is a requirement for ministers to go to Brussels

> "authorised to take binding decisions for the government of that member state..."

thus turning the British parliament into a glorified rubber stamp. But the most outrageous sign of the impotence of the British parliament was in the declaration by Foreign Secretary Hurd who, when it looked as if the Government was going to be defeated during the Maastricht ratification, claimed that defeat would have no effect since the government had committed the country under international treaty (see the Introduction for a discussion of royal prerogative).

The US government also displayed the kind of democratic credentials which have long disappeared from the United Kingdom in clause 2B(IV) of the GATT Bill which explicitly rejected any retrospective legislation affecting the states. How this contrasts with the British Government's retrospective pursuit of the property of freeholders forced to sell on demand to their leaseholders! The infamous "Barber" judgment of the European Court (on pension rights for men and women) imposed massive financial burdens on British industry, much of it retrospectively.

Most significant in preserving the sovereignty of the USA are the limitations under clause 3 whereby

> "no person other than the United States shall have any cause of action under any of the Uruguay Round Agreements."

This contrasts with the constant references to the "European Court of Justice" of the British government by sundry disgruntled individuals, politically motivated trade unions or pressure groups unable to achieve their aims within the United Kingdom by democratic means. If citizens of a nation can take their government (and even their Queen) to the court of another sovereignty to be judged under that institution's laws then can that nation truly be said to exist at all?

Commenting on this limitation of rights the Bill before the US Congress stated:

> "It is the intention of the Congress through (this) paragraph to occupy the field with respect to any cause of action or defence under or in connection with any of the Uruguay Round Agreements."

This "occupied field" principle is also part of European Community legislation ("acquis communautaire") but there it points precisely in the opposite direction ie it is the European Union which retains the rights to legislate exclusively in any field over which it has given a judgment. And of course the scope for such judgments is vast - because the political agreement of 12 countries was only possible through vague and ambiguous language of the kind which requires national judiciaries to refer constantly to the European Court.

So the United States has avoided in both the GATT and NAFTA agreements many of the pitfalls of the European Community Treaties - thus exposing, by contrast, the appalling irresponsibility of the British government. But it remains to be seen whether the legal assurances which the US Congress has given itself will stand up to the developing power of the new GATT "World Trade Organisation" and the stringency of international legal judgments when disputes over US sovereignty arise. If the British experience is any guide the USA has taken a very great risk with its (assumed) right to self governance.

3.

TREASONABLE ASPECTS OF THE MAASTRICHT TREATY

"EC Legislation is automatically part of our laws -
Parliament has no role to play."
The Hansard Society

The United Kingdom is a democracy and a monarchy. The two pivotal powers are **the people** from whom democracy derives and **the Queen** who is the Head of State and as whose subjects the people enjoy their identity and freedoms. Parliament and Government are mere functionaries and intermediaries in the democratic process. They neither represent the State nor are they the ultimate source of democratic justification. Power is delegated to them by the people for limited periods. Indeed since the people can throw out their Government, while the Government cannot throw out the people, there is no doubt who is sovereign and therefore - normally - in control.

But these are not normal times and the Maastricht Treaty - negotiated and signed by **Government** - turns the British **people** into an 8% minority (in the Council of Ministers) and a 15.3% minority (in the European Parliament), in virtually all decisions affecting their lives. "The Queen in Parliament" is losing all democratic content. The Treaty completely changes the positions of the Queen and her subjects both towards the EEC and in their relationship with each other. **The Government has made the Queen and her subjects**

(without their consent) citizens of an alien power towards which they will have duties and by whom they can be taxed. This is in moral and political terms (and possibly in legal terms) treason since the sovereign has been subordinated to a foreign authority and the British constitution has been fatally undermined.

There are certain critical principles in the constitution of every country (whether they have a written constitution or not) which can never be sacrificed, even after an overwhelming vote. It is on just such grounds that the German Government found itself arraigned before its own Federal Constitutional Court. For although two thirds majorities in both Houses of the German parliament are sufficient to change the constitution in most respects, certain basic principles - like one man one vote, or that Germany is governed by Germans - **are absolutely inviolable.** (In the event as we shall see, below, the Court's approval seemed to have nothing to do with the actual terms of the Treaty as signed!) Even without a formal constitution in the United Kingdom a series of critical laws and conventions, combined with the powerful loyalties of the British people, represent a strong bulwark against constitutional betrayal.

The extent to which the Maastricht Treaty betrays the very foundation of the British peoples' laws and rights is demonstrated by those British laws which will be broken by our ratification of the treaty. The 1932 case law which stipulates that "no Parliament may bind its successors" is broken since the Treaty permits no withdrawal from this "irrevocable" and "irreversible" Union and stipulates that the "treaty is concluded for an unlimited period". Of even greater moment is the lack of any right of or mechanism for secession from this "European Union". This is precisely the reason given by President Lincoln (inaugural address 4th March 1861) for justifying war against the southern states which wished to leave the American Union. He noted that "No state upon its own mere motion can lawfully get out of the Union". It was this and not the question of slavery (for which Lincoln expressed accommodation in his address) which was the principal cause of the American civil war which cost 600,000 lives.

According to the **Act of Settlement (1700)** no one may stand for Parliament in the United Kingdom unless they are of British nationality. But the Maastricht Treaty permits those who do not enjoy this status (ie all EEC citizens) to vote and stand in elections for our national (Westminster) Parliament. Although "European citizens" are described as having the right to vote in "municipal elections" it is quite clear from court cases and judgments in the United Kingdom and Europe that the word "municipal" means national - and not "local" (as the British Government interprets the word). An example from the European Court in 1972 both makes this definition clear and shows how the nation states of Europe must be subordinated to the new European superstate:

> "the treaty entails a definitive limitation of the sovereign rights of member states against which no provisions of municipal law, whatever their nature, can be invoked."

This is a classic case of how the definitions of words on which the British Government is relying to increase our national powers of self government are used by Eurofederalists to confirm the hegemony of the Euro-state. "Subsidiarity" for instance is a federalist expression which merely allows the centre in Brussels to delegate subordinate tasks to the peripheral nation states. As Lady Thatcher rightly pointed out in the House of Lords debate (see below) The European Commission emphasised

> "The enshrinement of subsidiarity in the Treaty provided an opportunity to stress that subsidiarity cannot be used to bring the Commission to heel by challenging its right of initiative and in this way alter the balance established by the Treaty."

Indeed the wording of the treaty is quite clear - that the "acquis communautaire" (the existing body of European law) must be preserved. Douglas Hurd himself, in conversation with Rodney Atkinson, admitted that Maastricht did not give back to Britain one iota of sovereignty. This the Foreign Secretary admitted while the Prime Minister was selling the Treaty on the basis that some elements of sovereignty at least were being returned. Nothing could be further from the truth. Even Hurd's assertion that in future more decisions would be taken in the United Kingdom has been shown to be fraudulent as the British Government is powerless to stop laws on trade unions, workers rights, maternity pay and working hours being imposed above the heads of our own Parliament.

It is the European Union which will decide what powers and responsibilities will and will not be delegated to what remains of the sovereign nations of Europe. Any conflict between European institutions and the British Government on this issue will be referred to the European Court which has made its federalist goals explicit on several occasions.

The oath sworn by the Queen under the 1953 Coronation Oaths Act commits Her Majesty to "govern the peoples of the United Kingdom according to their laws and customs". But by no stretch of the imagination could laws formulated by the Brussels Commission or the Strasbourg Parliament where the British are in a fixed minority, be described as "their laws". It is totally inconceivable that laws formulated by the European Court as **the sole interpreter** of words in the Rome Treaties, could ever be described as **our** laws. It can never have been the intention of the formulators of the coronation oath or of Her Majesty the Queen who swore it, that "the Queen in Parliament" should rubber stamp **without power to annul or alter** (see Article 192) an average of 27 directives per day from an alien power. As the Hansard Society noted in a recent annual report on the proceedings of Parliament:

> "EC legislation is automatically part of a member state's laws. Parliament, strictly speaking, has no role to play except in the implementation of directives."

One of the many advantages of a monarchy is that the nation state and its sovereignty are embodied in the person of the Queen, her heirs and successors. Not only does the Maastricht

Treaty turn the British people into citizens of another country (what else could this "European Union" be, which already possesses courts, parliament, passport, civil service, flag and even a national anthem?) **but the Queen herself becomes a "citizen" of this other country.** Following the ratification of the Maastricht Treaty the Queen, like her subjects, has duties towards this "European Union" (Article 8). According to the Foreign Office the Queen can vote in local elections in other EEC states and EEC elections! **In other words the Queen, under Maastricht, becomes a citizen not a monarch. In fact, like other citizens, the Queen will be open to be taxed by the "European" Union** (Article 192 of the integrated treaty). This article is a particularly potent example of how the decisions of the European Council or Commission can be imposed directly on British citizens "without other formality than verification of the authenticity of the decision" and **outside** "the jurisdiction of the courts of the country concerned".

The Government claims that these European rights are purely "voluntary", the duties are non-existent and citizenship, we are told, does not **mean** citizenship. And yet we cannot opt out of our rights, nor our duties, nor our citizenship - **and neither can Her Majesty the Queen.**

It is quite clear that Ministers of the Crown have subordinated Her Majesty to an alien power over which the British people have no control. **Despite the protestations of British Ministers about the "true" meaning of words in the Treaty, it will be the European Court, not the British Government, which decides those meanings and that Court has defined its duty as "enabling the Community interest to prevail over the inertia and resistance of member states".**

In other words the European Court of Justice is not a court at all in the normal sense of the word but a functionary in a political process.

The Queen's sovereignty has been replaced by her **suzerainty**. In this new position of **suzerainty (the sovereign of a state**

which cannot act independently because another state holds supremacy over it) the Queen herself embodies the powerlessness of the British people and Parliament within this new "European Union". The Foreign Office argues that the duties imposed on the British people are not specific. But nothing could be more onerous and specific than the duty to pay taxes. As the British people and Government will soon recognise, any attempt to remove or change the 17.5% VAT on fuel will be illegal under European rules. There are in addition many general and wide ranging duties imposed on individuals (like the obligation to carry a "European" passport) and on our Parliament (to obey the Commission and the European Court which is now given even more areas of "common policy" over which to adjudicate).

Under Article 8a all EEC citizens have the right to move to the UK and enjoy the same rights as those who have British nationality. The Portuguese Government, for instance, has made the citizens of Macao Portuguese nationals who therefore become European citizens and have right of entry into the United Kingdom. This contrasts with the exclusion of most citizens of Hong Kong from British nationality and therefore European citizenship. **It is possible that over a period of, say, 50 years a large minority of those living in Britain will have no interest in and acceptance of the Queen as their Head of State, not least since they will not share British nationality.** This will represent a truly "alien wedge" of citizens with far less allegiance to the British crown than, say, Commonwealth citizens. Indeed many will come from countries which spent many years of the 20th century attempting to conquer Her Majesty's territories.

One of the most incredible aspects of the Maastricht Treaty is the almost complete loss of immigration control by the British Government. Article 100c states that, from 1st January 1996 "The Council, acting by majority voting, shall determine the third countries whose nationals must be in possession of a visa when crossing the external borders of the member states." In other words other EC countries will be deciding who and under what visa conditions, shall enter the United Kingdom.

Even more incredibly the "Declaration on nationality of a member state" states that the sole right of decision on nationality **lies with each individual member state**. With each EC national enjoying European citizenship and the right "to move and reside freely" within the Union it is quite clear that the British people and their Parliament will have no right to determine the numbers or identity of non British nationals to whom other member states can give residence and voting rights in the United Kingdom.

It is also evident that the first and possibly most important statute in British constitutional history, the Magna Carta, (last reviewed on the passing of the 1967 Statute Repeals Act) contains the following which is hardly compatible with the provisions of the Maastricht Treaty:

> "No freeman may be...disseised...of his liberties or free customs...nor will we not pass upon him but by the law of the land."

Neither the daily deluge of Brussels directives nor the law creating activities of the European Court could ever be described as the law of our country. The British Government claims that since British laws approve, post factum, the impositions of the European Community then these European laws are therefore British laws. But the definition of a British law is one which originates in a manifesto of a party triumphant at the polls, is framed by our own legislators and is then passed into law by our own Parliament. Any other process or any appeals to some blanket provision in the European Communities Act 1972 (about which the then Government told blatant lies), the 1986 Single European Act or the Maastricht Treaty - neither of which were expressly approved by the British electorate - are democratically, and therefore constitutionally, invalid.

In the United Kingdom police officers and members of the armed services, as part of their contract of employment, swear allegiance to the Queen. The police swear to serve "Our Sovereign Lady the Queen" and "prevent all offences against the persons and properties of Her Majesty's subjects". The armed services swear "allegiance to her Majesty Queen Elizabeth, Her Heirs and Successors...in person crown and dignity against all enemies.." However it is quite clear under Maastricht that the police will no longer have a sovereign Queen to defend, but a Queen subordinated to another power. They will also have to defend many thousands of citizens (from other EEC countries) who are NOT Her Majesty's subjects. **The Maastricht Treaty therefore effectively causes the violation of the policeman's oath.**

Similarly the armed services, under Article J will in many circumstances not be serving the Queen (to whom they have sworn allegiance) and her subjects but the President of the "European Union" **who will represent European defence policy**. Under Article J1 Britain and its armed services "shall refrain from any action contrary to the interests of the union" and (just to show that this is no voluntary process!!) "The Council shall ensure that these principles are complied with". This loss of sovereignty covers **"all areas of foreign and defence policy"**. This in no way equates with Britain's obligations towards NATO which was founded for the defence of **sovereign** states against a **specific** aggressor - the Soviet Union.

Admittedly, before British armed forces and policies become the subject of majority voting, a given policy area must, by unanimous vote, have been turned into an area of "common action". But once that has happened then British forces and British policy makers are powerless to conduct or change that policy. Incredibly the Foreign Secretary Douglas Hurd recently asked by a journalist to describe a possible area for "common action" said "Well, we could turn relations with the Soviet Union into an area of common action". But in any case even allowing for the apparent safeguard of unanimous voting, the

41

mere fact that it has been agreed that an institution like the "European Union" with its council, civil service, parliament, flag and even national anthem has conceived of common policies on defence and foreign affairs means that the pressure to "fall into line" or "not rock the boat" or to trade off concessions in other policy areas for agreement on foreign affairs all seriously jeopardise the clear defence of British interests through a specific, nationally defined British policy.

Can those who have subordinated the Queen to another power rely on the loyalty of the forces of law and order who have sworn allegiance to Her Majesty? Indeed may not those very politicians through their approval of the Maastricht Treaty, be guilty of treason (**"violation by a subject of his allegiance to his sovereign or to a state"**) since a Minister of the Crown must, like every MP, Privy Counsellor and member of the House of Lords, swear a similar oath of allegiance?

The British people know that something is very wrong with the Maastricht Treaty. They may not grasp the niceties of constitutional law but they do understand allegiance and that the invidious position of Her Majesty the Queen reflects their own powerlessness as the historic rights and traditions of their Parliament are thrown away.

4.

THE TREASON CASES LAID BEFORE THE COURTS IN ENGLAND AND SCOTLAND

The following are the charges which Rodney Atkinson and Norris McWhirter laid before the magistrates court in Hexham, Northumberland on 9th September 1993, under "Misprision of Treason".

The procedure of "misprision" is applicable to those who know of acts of either treason or terrorism and who, in the event that they did NOT report them to the proper authorities, would themselves be guilty of those crimes.

All the "informations" laid before the magistrates were preceded by the following words:

> "It being an offence at Common Law (see Halsbury 4th edition vol 11 at 818) for a person who knows that treason is being planned or committed, not to report the same as soon as he can to a justice of the peace we hereby lay the following information."

CASE 1:

Whereas it is an offence under Section 1 of the treason Act 1795 "within the realm or without...to devise...constraint of the person of our sovereign...his heirs or successors."

On 7th February 1992 the Rt Hon Douglas Richard Hurd, Secretary of State for Foreign and Commonwealth Affairs, King Charles Street, London SW1 and the Rt Hon the Hon Francis Anthony Aylmer Maude at that date Financial

43

Secretary to the Treasury, HM Treasury, Parliament Street, London SW1 did sign a Treaty of European Union at Maastricht in the Netherlands, according to Article 8 of which Her Majesty the Queen becomes a citizen of the European Union (confirmed by the Home Secretary in the House of Commons: Hansard 1st February 1993) therefore "subject to the duties imposed thereby", subject to being arraigned in her own courts and being taxed under Article 192 of the integrated Treaty and thereby effectively deposed as the sovereign and placed in a position of suzerainty under the power of the "European Union".

Therefore the said Rt Hon Douglas Hurd and the said Rt Hon the Hon Francis Maude are guilty of treason.

CASE 2:

Whereas it is an offence under section 1 of the Treason Act 1795 to engage in actions "tending to the overthrow of the laws, government and happy constitution" of the United Kingdom.........etc Hurd and Maude....etc did sign a Treaty of European Union...according to Article 8 of which "every person holding the nationality of a member state shall be a citizen of the Union" and according to Article 8a of which such citizens "shall have the right to move and reside freely within the territory" of any member state and according to Article 8b of which such citizens shall have the right to vote and according to which "Declaration on nationality" in the Final Act "the question whether an individual posesses the nationality of a member state shall be settled solely by reference to the national law of the member state concerned."

And that therefore the British people and Parliament will have no right to determine the numbers or identity of non British nationals to whom other European Union member states can give residence rights and voting rights in the United Kingdom.

And whereas according to the Act of Settlement 1700 s4 "The Laws of England are the birthright of the People".

And whereas Sir Robert Megarry (Blackburn v Attorney General, Chancery Division 1983 Ch77,89) has stated that

> "And as a matter of law the courts of England recognise Parliament as being omnipotent in all save the power to destroy its omnipotence."

Therefore the said Rt Hon Douglas Hurd and the said Rt Hon the Hon Francis Maude are guilty of treason.

CASE 3:

Whereas it is an offence under the Act of Settlement (1700) for any "person born out of the Kingdoms of England, Scotland or Ireland or the Dominions thereunto...shall be capable to be...a Member of either House of Parliament"

And whereas according to R v Thistlewood 1820 "to destroy the constitution of the country" is an act of treason.

And whereas the term "municipal" has been defined by the European Court of Justice in 1972 as meaning "national":

> "...the treaty entails a definitive limitation of the sovereign rights of member states against which no provisions of municipal law whatever their nature, can be involved."

and similarly defined by Lord Justice Cumming Bruce giving the majority verdict in McCarthys v Smith 1979 ICR 785,798:

> "If the terms of the Treaty (of Rome) are adjudged in Luxembourg to be inconsistent with the provisions of the Equal Pay Act 1970, European Law will prevail over that municipal legislation"

Hurd and Maude...etc did sign a Treaty ....etc according to Article 8b of which "Every citizen of the Union residing in a member state of which he is not a national shall have the right to vote and stand as a candidate at municipal elections in the Member State in which he resides."

Therefore the said Rt Hon Douglas Hurd and the said the Rt Hon Francis Maude are guilty of treason.

CASE 4:

Whereas the United Kingdom of Great Britain and Northern Ireland is a monarchy in which Her Majesty Queen Elizabeth II is sovereign and Head of State and a democracy, whereby the people of that United Kingdom rule by delegating their authority for periods of up to 5 years to the Parliament and Government in London.

And whereas, according to the Act of Settlement 1700 s4 "The laws of England are the birthright of the people"

And whereas Sir Robert Megarry (Blackburn v Attorney General, Chancery Division 1983 Ch 77,89) has stated that

> "As a matter of law the courts of England recognise Parliament as being omnipotent in all save the power to destroy its own omnipotence."

And whereas according to R v Thistlewood 1820 to "destroy the Constitution" is an act of treason.

.....Hurd and Maude...etc did sign a treaty...etc according to Article 8 of which the British people, without their consent have been made the citizens of the European Union with duties towards the same and according to Article 192 of the integrated treaty the British people can be taxed directly by that European Union without further process in the Westminster Parliament and according to Article 171 of which the British State can be forced to pay a monetary penalty to the European Union.

Therefore the said Rt Hon Douglas Hurd......etc

CASE 5:

Whereas, in accordance with the Coronation Oath Act, Her Majesty Queen Elizabeth II swore at Her Coronation in 1953 that she would govern Her subjects "according to their laws".

And whereas it is an offence under Section 1 of the Treason Act 1795 "within the realm or without...to devise...constraint of the person of our sovereign...his heirs or successors"

Hurd and Maude....etc did sign a Treaty....etc which extended the powers of the European Commission, the European Court of Justice and the European Parliament in the new "European Union" to make and enforce in the United Kingdom laws which do not originate in the Westminster Parliament. And that this loss of democratic rights was without the express consent of the British people.

And whereas, according to the Act of Settlement 1700 s4 "The Laws of England are the Birthright of the people"

And whereas Lord Justice Robert Megarry (Blackburn v Attorney General, Chancery Division 1983 Ch 77,89) has stated that

> "As a matter of law the courts of England recognise Parliament as being omnipotent in all save the power to destroy its omnipotence."

Therefore Hurd and Maude are guilty of treason....etc

CASE 6:

Whereas it was established in 1932 that "No Parliament may bind its successors" (Vauxhall Estates v Liverpool Corporation 1, KB 733)

And whereas according to R v Thistlewood 1820 to destroy the constitution is an act of treason.

Hurd and Maude etc ...did sign a Treaty...according to which Article Q of which the Maastricht Treaty "is concluded for an unlimited period" **and from which there is no right of nor mechanism for secession.**

Therefore Hurd and Maude are guilty of treason etc..

This is one of the more extraordinary aspects of the Maastricht Treaty since it provides a direct parallel with that other

"Union", the American Union signed by the Southern, confederate states on the assumption that they could leave that Union whenever they wished. But they had omitted to ensure that both the right to and mechanism for withdrawal were included specifically in the Union declaration. As a result, the American President Abraham Lincoln (inaugural address 4th March 1861) justified war against the southern states by saying:

> "No state upon its own mere motion can lawfully get out
> of the Union"

It was this issue and not the question of slavery (for which Lincoln had expressed accommodation in his inaugural address) which caused the American Civil War in which 364,511 died compared to only 4,435 in the American War of Independence (1775-1783). The northern states were engaged not on a moral crusade but on an imperialist adventure, using the industrial and military might of the North to conquer the largely rural, raw material producing South.

Although the European Union as yet possesses no significant armed forces, this is the ultimate intention and an embryo Franco-German force has already been set up. The possible exit from this "Union" of Britain, the second biggest paymaster, with the richest coal, oil and fishing reserves in Europe and with the world's largest investments in the American economy might one day tempt any new breed of Euro-fascist to use the logic of Abraham Lincoln.

CASE 7:

Whereas it is established by a statute in force, the Magna Carta (Chapter 29) confirmed in 1297 and last reviewed at the passing of the Statute Law Repeals Act 1967 that:

> "No freeman may be...disseised...of his liberties or free
> customs...nor will we not pass upon him but by the law of
> the land."

This most durable pillar of the constitution is destroyed by a "Treaty of European Union"...etc..which disseises all free men of their liberties and free customs under the law of this land by subjugating their Government to the extension of the powers of the European Commission, Court and parliament (in which latter the United Kingdom members form a minority of 87 of 567 voting members). Under Article 192 of the integrated treaty our free men are open to be taxed without further process of the United Kingdom Parliament and according to the "Declaration on nationality" in the Final Act of the treaty the number and identity of non British nationals given residence and voting rights in the United Kingdom will not be determined by the British Government. And further that the treaty extends majority voting in the Council of Ministers thus permitting other states to determine laws which govern British people. Under Article 8 of the Treaty free men are required to become citizens of the European Union "subject to the duties imposed thereby."

And whereas according to R v Thistlewood 1820 "to destroy the constitution" is an act of treason.

Therefore Hurd and Maude....etc

CASE 8 (IN SCOTLAND):

Whereas it is an offence per s1 of the Treason Act 1795:

> "within the realm or without...to devise....constraint of the person of our sovereign...his heirs or successors."

and

> "to enter into measures tending to the overthrow of the laws, government and happy constitution of the United Kingdom"

and whereas to destroy the constitution per R v Thistlewood 1820 is an act of treason.

Hurd and Maude etc...did sign a treaty....for an unlimited period and without right of or mechanism for secession. This treaty is contrary to and inconsistent with the Union with Scotland Act 1706 whereby it is established per Article III of that Act the people of the United Kingdom be represented by the one and the same Parliament and none other and per Article XVIII that no alteration be made in laws which concern private right except for the evident utility of the subjects within Scotland.

Under the treaty, the rule of a Parliament other than that of the Parliament of the United Kingdom is established whereunder, contrary to the Act of Union, subjects within Scotland become subject to laws made in an assembly in which their representatives form a minority seven fold more slender than in the parliament of the United Kingdom.

Therefore Hurd and Maude....etc

CONCLUSION

Since the United Kingdom has no formal codified constitution in the manner of the USA or Germany, we rely on certain critical statutes and precedents in case law to formalise and hold fast for future generations the wisdom of the laws which have established and guaranteed our rights and liberties and the institutions of Parliament, Government and Courts.

It is one of the major safeguards for the people that past rights are enshrined in **specific** statutes and **specific** clauses. Imprecise words, confused sentences and contradictory clauses are a danger since they allow potential tyrants to exploit or bypass uncertainty in the law. It has therefore always been accepted as vital that any repeal of a statute or part of a statute should be made specific in new legislation. This is not just to "tidy up" the law books but more important so that everyone - voters, Parliament, ministers and journalists should know precisely how their historic guarantees are being affected.

But in the text of the Maastricht Bill layed before Parliament there was no mention of any of the many contraventions of historical statutes by the terms of the Treaty. The only reference to another Act of Parliament was to that of the 1978 European Parliamentary Elections Act, the terms of which would have been contradicted had a specific Parliamentary approval not been obtained.

The British people were deliberately kept in the dark about the destruction of their constitution and how the Maastricht Treaty and the European Community Amendments Act effectively threw out many of the most important statutes in British Parliamentary history. The first strategy of the tyrant is secrecy. The second is to lose the detail in a mass of superficiality and generalisation. Both were evident in the passage of the Maastricht Treaty Bill.

Some statutes within the British system of an informal constitution could perhaps, at some stretch of the imagination, be regarded as less critical. But this could certainly not be said about the Union with Scotland Act, for in 1706 the Scottish people decided to share a Sovereign and a Parliament. Since the new Parliament of the UNITED Kingdom was to be in England (and the physical existence of the Scottish parliament dispensed with)the terms of the Act of Union were absolutely vital. The Act is the nearest we possess to an actual constitution. The Scots, effectively, gave up their Parliament only in return for the guarantee that the new (English dominated) Parliament would not curtail or in any way diminish their rights. If they did so (as has now happened under the Maastricht Treaty) then the Act of Union would be null and void and not only would the United Kingdom cease to exist but so would the authority of the Parliament at Westminster which was spawned by the Act of Union.

This is exactly what has happened and the British people, once the full enormity of the betrayal has dawned upon them, will exact a terrible revenge on those who purport to be their "democratic representatives".

5.

REPLY TO THE CROWN PROSECUTION SERVICE

David Kyle Esq
Crown Prosecution Service
Headquarters
50 Ludgate Hill
London EC4M 7EX

1st November 1993

Dear Mr Kyle,

I am in receipt of a copy of your letter to Miss P.Axon, Clerk to the Justices, Hexham Magistrates Court dated 22 October. You have decided not to take further action on the 7 cases against two Government Ministers under "misprision of treason", laid before the said magistrates on 9th September 1993 by myself and Norris McWhirter.

Your first paragraph of 2. suggests that somehow Ministers are not responsible individually for their actions, just because they are carrying out Government policies. It is however well established in law that in the exercise of such powers Ministers must obey the law and such precedents as the "M case" (Kenneth Baker) and the 1977 Laker Airways case demonstrate this.

You argue that treaty making powers are vested in the Government, exercising prerogative powers. However **it was** made quite clear by the Government - and by your letter - that the basis of the ratification was not the use of prerogative power but the Act of Parliament (the European Communities (Amendment) Act 1993).

Indeed had the Government relied on prerogative power, that power would have been used to constrain the Sovereign, (the Government and the Crown being quite clearly two separate constitutional entities) which would have been a new prerogative power. According to the Statute of Proclamations NO NEW PREROGATIVE POWERS MAY BE CREATED. Therefore no such power was created and therefore the prerogative was not the source of legitimacy for the Maastricht Treaty.

So the authority for the signing of the Maastricht Treaty was the European Communities (Amendment) Act 1993. **But at the time of the signing of the Treaty that Act had not been passed. Therefore the two Ministers had no authority to sign on behalf of the British people and , there being no immunities included in the Bill, they are guilty of treason. I therefore ask you to consider legal proceedings on those grounds.**

Furthermore if there was a requirement to include in the Act a section specifically referring to the requirements of the 1978 European Parliamentary Elections Act then **why were there no sections specifically repealing the many statutes referred to in our submissions as being contravened by the treaty?**

Yours Sincerely

Rodney E.B. Atkinson

6.

MAASTRICHT AND UK GENERAL ELECTIONS

Following the refusal of the prosecuting authorities in England and Scotland to proceed with the Treason cases, Rodney Atkinson instigated questions to the Government in the House of Lords on some of the matters covered by those unanswered cases. The following press release was issued on 1st November 1993:

MAASTRICHT TREATY PREVENTS GOVERNMENT FROM DECIDING WHO CAN VOTE IN GENERAL ELECTIONS

GOVERNMENT REPLIES TO QUESTIONS IN HOUSE OF LORDS

TREATY DESTROYS QUEENS CORONATION OATH

In reply to a written question in the House of Lords by Lord Stoddart of Swindon, the Government has admitted that it does not have the right to decide whether any of the 283m "European Citizens" who are not British have the right to vote in British general elections.

Lord Stoddart had asked what advice the Government had received on the interpretation of the word "municipal" where it is used in the Maastricht Treaty to allow any of the 283 million EC nationals to vote in the "municipal elections" of the United Kingdom in so far as they are resident here.

Despite detailed and irrefutable evidence from both the European Court of Justice and the British courts that the word "municipal" means "national" the Government claims that "municipal elections" mean "local elections".

In reply to a further question **the Government admitted that neither they nor the British Parliament would determine what "municipal" meant. It would be the European Court of Justice which would decide who could or could not vote in a British general election.**

A further question put by Lord Stoddart asked

> "Whether increased powers given to European Institutions and the extension of majority voting in the Council of Ministers under the Maastricht Treaty will place Her Majesty the Queen in contravention of her Coronation Oath whereby Her Majesty swore to govern her subjects **"according to their laws." "**

In replying that this was not the case Baroness Chalker completely contradicted the Government's answer to Lord Stoddart on the "municipal" question.

Earl Ferrers, on behalf of the Government, had admitted that neither the British Government nor the British Parliament could decide the meaning of municipal and that **the European Court of Justice would, by its judgment, make the law in the United Kingdom. And it would do so on the most basic question of all in a democratic society - by deciding who can vote in elections to our national Parliament.**

This means that Her Majesty the Queen cannot govern her subjects "according to their laws" and that on its own admission the Government has caused Her Majesty the Queen to breach her Coronation Oath.

Rodney Atkinson, who with Norris McWhirter, laid treason charges against Government Ministers for signing the Maastricht Treaty, said that **"these Government answers in the House of Lords clearly show how grave is the constitutional crisis facing the people of the United Kingdom. Her Majesty the Queen, like the British people has been betrayed by the Government. Government Ministers responsible for negotiating and signing the Maastricht Treaty should resign forthwith."**

When, after much effort, it was possible to interest a British journalist in the threat to the constitution of our country, the result was an extraordinary public indictment of the dangerous incompetence of the British Foreign Office.

It was Boris Johnson of the *Sunday Telegraph* who took up the issue raised in the above press release with a spokesman from the Foreign Office. His report in the Sunday Telegraph of 20th November 1993 described how

> "Maastricht breaks ground in allowing all EEC citizens to vote and stand for "municipal" elections. What might these be exactly ? Are general elections excluded? 'There is some focus on the word municipal' admitted a Government source yesterday."

This "focus" it must be noted occured some two and a half years after the Maastricht Treaty was originally signed and months after the Government (too late for the General Election which Major claims approved the Treaty) had published the Treaty. Boris Johnson's article went on:

> "One British official, who offered, in a tired, kindly way to look it up while we were talking on the telephone, was brought up short by the Oxford English Dictionary. 'Oh' he said 'Hmmmm....pertaining to the internal affairs of a state as opposed to its foreign relations.' The risk is that no matter how the Government chooses to interpret the eventual directive defining "municipal" a Greek socialist, say, on being refused the right to stand as MP for Minehead, could take up the dispute in the European Court. And who knows where that would lead?"

In fact we know precisely where that would lead since we have examples of the Court's own use of the word municipal to mean "national" (see Treason case 3).

7.

LADY THATCHER AND LORD TONYPANDY - SPEECHES IN THE HOUSE OF LORDS

Dissident Tory and Independent Peers launched powerful attacks on the Maastricht Bill during its passage through the House of Lords. The extracts from the day's debate on 7th June, reproduced below, include trenchant speeches by the former Speaker of the House of Commons, Viscount Tonypandy (formerly George Thomas), and Margaret Thatcher (former Prime Minister), both of which draw attention to the fundamental change in our constitution and the loss of sovereignty and self-government enshrined in the Maastricht Treaty.

Viscount Tonypandy:

My lords, your Lordsbips will be aware that during the decade that I have been privileged to serve in your Lordships' House I have very carefully avoided speaking on what I considered to be clearly party political issues. Following the precedent of others who have been Speaker of the House of Commons, I have endeavoured to speak on those issues which are not clearly belonging to one side or the other. I believe that the destiny of the British people is bigger than any party and that this House has an equal responsibility with the other House to give careful consideration to what is at stake.

First, I am of the opinion that those who support Maastricht and those who oppose it will agree that the course for Britain will never be the same again if this treaty is ratified.

Because I believe that the sovereignty of our country is at stake I feel obliged to address your Lordships' House and say this: power under Maastricht it to be transferred from the elected representatives of our people to Europe where we will be a permanent minority. Tell our unemployed to go to Germany and look for a job; to go to Italy to look for a job and to go to France to look for a job. They will look to the High Court of Parliament here to take the economic measures that we believe are in our national interest. I say with respect to the noble Lord on the Government Front Bench, that his speech was the least enthusiastic of the three to which I have listened.

Since we joined the Community we have had a net trading deficit of no less than £81 billion to which might be added a net deficit in our Community contributions of over £13 billion, making all told a deficit for this country with the Community since we joined of the best part of £95 billion. It is interesting to note that 70 per cent of the world's trade is still conducted between English-speaking countries. The noble Lord, Lord Jenkins of Hillhead, scolded the noble Baroness who is to follow me in this debate for quoting Clem Attlee. Perhaps I may quote what Winston Churchill said in 1953. Many a time that great leader of our nation was prophetic both before the war and during the war. I served on the opposite Benches to him for 15 years in another place. He said:

> "We are with Europe but not of it. We are linked but not comprised. We are associated but not absorbed. And should European statesmen address us and say, 'Shall we speak for thee?', we should reply, 'Nay Sir, for we dwell among our own people".

The long proud history of the House of Commons and of your Lordships' House is very precious. The dignity of our nation is wrapped up in the history of our people. Therefore, who should decide? Scorn has been poured on a referendum, yet the noble Lord, Lord Callaghan will know that we had a referendum over the piffling issue of that non-legislative assembly in Wales. It was thought essential. Parliament could not decide. The Government decided that the people must decide because the constitution was affected. We all know that the constitution is very much affected today.

In the first referendum that took us into Europe we had an assurance from all the leaders that our sovereignty would never be in question. We have been led inch by inch and now they tell us that we have gone too far and that we cannot pull back. I believe in this country and I believe that the British people are equal with the French and the Danes in their ability to measure where their interests lie. This is a matter where the High Court of Parliament should say to the people, "This is our advice and because we are deciding for those yet unborn, let the people as a whole decide." Britain wants a referendum and she deserves it.

Baroness Thatcher:

... I believe very much, with the noble Viscount Lord Tonypandy, that it does not matter where we sit in this House; it does not matter where we work in the country or what our party politics are; it is our country's future that is at stake. It is our parliamentary institutions. It is our court of law. We called ourselves "free people" long before we had a universal vote in this country because we had the most excellent rule of law - and that matters to us very much.

If one looks back and tries to view things in a broad sweep, one finds that there have always been two views of Europe: one is of nation states freely co-operating together with an effective veto either by unanimity or by the Luxembourg Compromise - and of course, majority voting did not start with the Single European Act; it is right in the Treaty of Rome. That is why De Gaulle had the Luxembourg Compromise - because he quarrelled with something which would otherwise have been done by majority voting. The Luxembourg Compromise acted as a veto ...

The second view has always been towards an integrated European union. That is why the phrase an "ever closer union" was put in the Treaty of Rome - not clothed with meaning. We always had the assurance to which my noble friend referred. There was always an assurance that we would keep our identity and our veto but gradually, little by little, it went and everything came in stages. Whatever you said in the Community, it had to be the first stage of something which led to one destination, a European union. You did not have any other alternatives. You were either on a slow train or a fast train, but you were on the train to that destination - and if you do not want to go to that destination, it does not matter at what speed you go. You do not want to go any further on that train ...

The Maastricht Treaty extends the powers of the Commission from 11 to 20 areas of government and provides for 111 new occasions when decisions can be by qualified majority. This is a massive extension ... Some of those majority occasions include decisions in economic and monetary policy. This is an overwhelming centralisation of decisions by bureaucracy at the expense of democracy and at the expense of accountability to the electorate.

Perhaps I may say a word about subsidiarity, a topic to which my noble friend referred. The Treaty talks about subsidiarity, and then it immediately confirms the present corpus of law (the *acquis communautaire*). So subsidiarity does not go to any regulations or directives which are already in being. The Commission's view on subsidiarity is put very interestingly in a long document presented to the Council and Parliament. The Commission points out in that document:

> "The enshrinement of subsidiarity in the Treaty (of Maastricht)...provided an opportunity to stress that subsidiarity cannot be used to bring the Commission to

heel by challenging its right of initiative and in this way altering the balance established by the Treaties".

The Edinburgh Summit communique said something similar. It said:

"The principle of subsidiarity does not relate to and cannot call into question the powers conferred on the European Community by the Treaty as interpreted by the Court...The application of the principle shall respect the general provisions of the Maastricht Treaty including maintaining in full the acquis communautaire and it shall not affect the primacy of Community law nor shall it call into question the principle set out in Article F(3) of the Treaty.... according to which the Union shall provide itself with the means to attain its objectives and carry through its policies."

I suggest respectfully that that is...a great move, as the noble Lord said, towards much greater centralisation.

I shall say a word about the European Court because it has had a great effect upon the powers that we have relinquished. It has by its decisions greatly extended the powers of the centralised institutions against the nation state. Its methods of interpreting the law are totally different from those of our courts and nothing like so exact or so good. The Court draws upon the objective of European integration to inform all its rulings by which over a period of time it has therefore furthered decisions towards a unitary European State.

The Court has also overruled specific legislation passed in good faith through Parliament recently (the Merchant Shipping Act 1988) which was framed to stop Spanish fishing vessels from quota-hopping; that is, taking part of our fishing quota under the common fisheries policy. That Act went overboard because by some strange device the Court said that Community law overrode it. Even though it was recent, we did not prevail. It is busy reinterpreting so many things to give itself and the Community more powers at our expense...

Moreover, only three out of 13 judges of the European Court have judicial experience in their own countries. Perhaps that explains a lot! They all have legal qualifications: some have been Ministers; some have been senior civil servants. But we are used to having proper judges. Further, one judgement only is issued. We do not even know whether any judges dissented - we are not allowed to know - let alone upon what grounds. We, with our ancient court traditions and ancient rule of justice have far more to lose in this matter than any other country, many of which we doubt will respect some of the Community laws in any respect. Perhaps I may make some additional comments on the Maastricht Treaty before coming to the referendum. It starts in clear terms:

> "By this Treaty, the High Contracting Parties establish among themselves a European Union...This Treaty marks a new state in the process of creating an ever closer union".

There it is - straight out a new stage. It is a very important big step, because it seeks a new political entity, something we have never had before. It creates a European Union. Later, Article 8 creates a citizenship of the Union - something totally new. It establishes it. It applies to every person holding the nationality of a member state.

The Article refers to rights and duties and spells out the new rights which can be extended. Moreover, if there is a citizenship, you would all owe a duty of allegiance to the new Union. What else is citizenship about? There will be a duty to uphold its laws. What will happen if the allegiance to the Union comes into conflict with allegiance to our own country? How would the European Court find then? The Maastricht Treaty gives this new European Union all the attributes of a sovereign state.

I shall go through those attributes quickly. What are the attributes of a sovereign state? First, there is citizenship. It gives the right to conduct foreign policy and assert its identity on the international scene (the whole of this Treaty has that); and the right to frame a common defence policy which in time could lead to common defence (the Treaty has that). It has its own Supreme Court of Justice, the guardian of its constitution. It has its own external boundaries. It manages its own economic and monetary policy. It will have its own central bank, ultimately including a single currency, hopefully not including us, although we have signed up to the idea of a single currency. It has a single market. It conducts its international trade negotiations as a unit. We have no authority to conduct trade negotiations. We lost that in 1972. We have signed up to the objective of a high level of social protection. I wonder whether the Social Chapter will be brought in by the European Court to apply to Britain, because we have signed up to that high level of social protection. There is an embryo government in the Council of Ministers (the European Council); there is an executive in the Commission; and there is an elected European Parliament. All of that is "the single institutional framework" to which the Treaty refers.

The voluntary alliance of 12 nations that we joined is being turned gradually into a new political entity - a European superstate. I doubt very much whether the people realise what is happening.

I could never have signed this Treaty. I hope that that is clear to all who have heard me. The Bill will pass considerable further powers irrevocably from Westminster to Brussels, and, by extending majority voting, will undermine our age-old parliamentary and legal institutions, both far older than those in the Community. We have so much more to lose by this Maastricht Treaty than any other state in the European Community. It will diminish democracy and increase bureaucracy.

M. Delors knew well the importance of his words when he spoke to the European Parliament in 1988. He said:

> "Ten years hence, 80% of our economic legislation, and perhaps even ourfscal and social legislation as well, will be of Community origin".

He went on, and this is not so generally known:

"In 10 countries, though" -

we were excluded -

"there has been no realisation of this, and in these same 10 countries there is no co-operation between European parliamentarians and national parliaments".

Then he went on:

"What I am afraid of is that some of these national parliaments are going to wake up with a shock one day, and that their outraged reaction will place yet more obstacles in the way of progress towards European Union".

The national parliaments are entitled to have an outraged reaction. They will soon be little more than an agency for the Commission and for the European Council.

Finally, the referendum. No elector in this country has been able to vote against Maastricht - none. It has been impossible to do so. I think that when one looks at the extent of the powers which are being handed over, it would be disgraceful if we denied them that opportunity. Yes, we waited with bated breath for both Danish referenda. They thought that people were bullied out of their first decision. So much for the unanimity rule.

Further, in the other place less than half the honourable Members voted for the Treaty. The electorate has not been able to vote and half the honourable Members in the other place - less than half; 292 out of some 650 - voted for the Treaty. We are in the Rome Treaty and in the Single European Act and we stay there. I believe that to hand over the people's parliamentary rights on the scale of the Maastricht Treaty without the consent of the people in a referendum would be to betray the trust - as guardians of the parliamentary institutions, and of the Constitution - that they have placed in us.

8.

CHURCHILL, EUROPE AND "THE BRITISH FAMILY OF NATIONS"

Winston Spencer Churchill left the Conservative Party over the issue of free trade, returning only when that great liberal, internationalist argument had been won. In metaphorical terms at least he "left" the Conservative party in the 1930s to warn of the threat of the rise of European fascism and the integration of the nations of Europe into a "continental system" dominated by Germany. Again, in a sense, he left his own country to appeal directly to the American nation (into which his father had married) to recognise the threat which German domination of Europe in the 1930s represented for the interests of the United States.

While his heart was undoubtedly with the English speaking peoples he never lost sight of the threat which a continental superpower, (committed to collectivist supranationalism) represented for the free nations of the world and for the anglo saxon system of international trade and commerce.

After the second war, as Churchill's biographer Martin Gilbert points out:

> "Churchill supported the Labour Government's caveat that Britain could not enter any European economic system from which the Commonwealth was excluded."

For Churchill "ties of blood, of sentiment and tradition and common interest unite us with the other members of the British family of nations." But Churchill was a realist about

Europe, the source of two horrendous, devastating world wars and after the second war he was anxious to unite the two concepts of a peaceful Europe of cooperating nations with their respective imperial ties.

> "The Strasbourg recommendations urged the creation of an economic system which will embrace not only the European States but all those other states and territories elsewhere which are associated with them."

He saw in Europe the need to establish an economically successful system on the one hand and provide a system of "collective responsibility for the defence of liberty" on the other - the principal purpose of which was to bind Germany into a peaceful Europe - a Europe of nations. Even in such a system of defence Churchill was highly sceptical about the dilution of national identities which would damage the loyalty of individual soldiers. And as the first to warn of the new threat of the communist block and the "iron curtain" he saw descending, it is quite clear that Churchill had in mind a NATO system, not an army of a federal superstate.

Churchill opposed European Federation and towards the end of his life opposed even the Common Market - probably not so much per se but because he knew to what loss of national sovereignty such an organisation would undoubtedly lead. Martin Gilbert in his biography:

> "Montgomery had been to see him and emerged from his meeting to announce that Winston was against our going into the Common Market. Winston told Edwina (his granddaughter) that Monty's behaviour was 'monstrous'".

"Monstrous" is hardly consistent with a denial, being more an expression of anger that his antipathy to a European Community had been publicised. But by far the most convincing and categorical statement of Churchill's view of Britain's potential part in a European Federation was as follows:

"But we have our own dream and our own task. We are with Europe but not of it. We are linked but not comprised. We are interested and associated but not absorbed."

For Churchill, the sovereign nation state was the supreme entity. Without nationhood there would be no loyalty, no allegiance, no identity, no rallying point in times of crisis and no vehicle for peaceful trade and communication with other nations.

Even when Churchill talked of a "United States of Europe" he made clear in the same breath that the United Kingdom, should merely act as "joint sponsors" of that union with the Russians and the Americans. It was quite clear that the need for reconciliation, mutual defence and growing economic stability were Churchill's aims and he thought such a union - at that stage, just after the war - a suitable vehicle for achieving the democratisation of Germany and recociliation with France. But Germany's astounding post war growth, its record of (if anything excessive) pacifism and the stability of its democracy would surely have convinved him that such a union was no longer necessary, even for continental Europe. He would also have recogised the growth in political instability and the rise of extremist politics which moves *towards* greater European Union have brought about since 1972 and in particular since 1986.

Churchill's enjoyment of his own national identity was all the more intense when he received the recognition of another nation. Three months after the failure of the Macmillan attempt to enter the European Common Market Churchill received the honorary citizenship of the United States. He said on that occasion:

"It is a remarkable comment on our affairs that the former Prime Minister of a great sovereign state should thus be received as an honorary citizen of another. I say "great sovereign state" with design and emphasis for I reject the view that Britain and the Commonwealth should now be relegated to a tame and minor role in the world."

Could anyone conceive that the speaker of these words could have consorted with the modern German government with its barely disguised contempt for the sovereign nation? - or at least other peoples' sovereign nations!

There is no doubt where Churchill would have stood today on the issue of the European Union. He would have opposed it, just as he would have opposed the 1972 legislation, framed by Geoffrey Howe, which set the British people on the dangerous path towards a European superstate and the extinction of its sovereign nationhood.

For Churchill's whole life was a long crusade against collective power, the external management of trade and the supranational management of nations and against the divorce of the British people from their "ties of blood and sentiment". He would have seen, as the liberal, free trading Atlanticist does today, that the torches of freedom, nationhood, law and democracy have rarely burned for long on the continent of Europe. And when they were extinguished it was Britain who stood alone until the free men of free nations came to fight by her side. At such times the British could look to a Nelson, a Wellington and a Churchill and above all in this century to their friends across the Atlantic.

If one man, more than any other, has embodied the identity, history and aspirations of the British nation and that principled combination of conservative nationhood and liberal economic internationalism, then that man is Winston Churchill. His spirit lives on, we must hope that the nation he loved and to which he devoted his life will survive this new threat from the continent of Europe.

9.

AN OPEN LETTER TO THE 445 PEERS WHO VOTED AGAINST THE RECENT MAASTRICHT REFERENDUM AMENDMENT

DESPITE being in possession of all the cogent constitutional arguments for a referendum, you voted to frustrate the desire of the great majority of the British people to be consulted about whether they wish to be ruled from Westminster or Brussels.

As anyone following the debate can see, you lost all the arguments but your vote was cast against democracy. Opinion polls demonstrate that more than two-thirds of the British public want to have a say as to whether to continue or end nine centuries of national independence and self-governance. You voted to hand over something you do not own - something for which 1,242,944 people died defending in the first half of this century - people who left behind countless widows and orphans. This total included forty five parliamentarians.

Harming rule of law

By refusing a referendum on Maastricht, you are helping to destroy the basis for the rule of law, which is government by consent. You justified that refusal by saying that we are governed not by referendums but by parliamentary democracy.

Yet it is you who have connived at the gradual erosion of our parliamentary democracy by allowing more and more power to be transferred to Brussels. You are in the process of placing the United Kingdom in thrall to a multinational, nine-language overseas parliament, and a bunch of unelected bureaucrats in the European Commission. By making the Queen a citizen of Europe, you, in effect, voted to end our monarchy. She will now be able to be arraigned in her own courts. You are also helping to foist upon all the citizens of this country, including the Queen, a new nationality which establishes duties that are undefined and to which they have never consented.

You have aided and abetted the reduction of our famous Westminster Parliament from its historic position as the legislature of a sovereign state, to being merely the headquarters of the subsidiary government of a region of a federal European superstate. You have transformed our judiciary from being the interpreters of the will of a sovereign parliament to being the interpreters of secondary and tertiary laws. You are also turning our Civil Service into bureaucratic policemen whose primary function is to enforce European laws, directives and regulations which the electorate have had no say in formulating and which they are constitutionally powerless to resist.

Future consequences

In the name of European peace, you have sown the seeds of future civil unrest, for the British people are not going to meekly obey obnoxious laws enforced by a parliament in which 480 Euro-MPs whom they did not elect can outvote over 87 British Euro-MPs (for whom there is little respect). The essence of democracy is to be ruled by people whom you can sack. We shall after Maastricht, be ruled by unsackable bureaucrats and, effectively unsackable Euro-MPs.

By voting to deny the British people a referendum, you are helping to destroy our Constitution. Few today may call it treason, but tomorrow many will.

Like sleep-walkers

Most of you are behaving like sleep-walkers in a vital hour for the life of our country. You should instead recall the words of the man who brought Britain through the last Continental attempt to neuter us and create a European empire. At a time when Churchill had only a tiny band of supporters, at a time when he was called a warmonger by the craven supporters of appeasement in the 1930s, and when the BBC monopoly excluded him from the airwaves for 28 consecutive months, he wrote: "I have watched this famous island descending incontinently, fecklessly, the stairway which leads to a dark gulf. It is a fine, broad stairway at the beginning, but after a bit the carpet ends." That carpet ended in a 'Not Content' lobby in a House which voted to turn itself into a museum.

10.

EC'S GROWING CONTROL
OF TAXATION

During the fierce battles over the ratification of the Maastricht Treaty, it became easy to lose sight of the many areas over which, Treaty or no Treaty, the European Community is quietly and steadily increasing its control over our lives.

Opponents of Maastricht, naturally enough, sought to portray the Treaty as a massive one-off transfer of sovereignty to Brussels. But in fact, many of the Treaty's more obnoxious provisions constituted no more than a belated official recognition of the de facto extension of EC authority into new areas. The worrying truth is that even had the Maastricht Treaty been defeated, the EC would have continued to expand its jurisdiction inexorably as it has done since it was set up. This is because of the so-called 'Occupied Field' doctrine: once the EC has legislated in a new area, its authority in that area is guaranteed in perpetuity. Known as the acquis communautaire, this steady and irreversible accumulation of power by the EC constitutes a one-way street to centralisation.

Centralist rachet

The growth in EC competence over indirect taxation is a textbook example of the centralist ratchet-effect. Article 99 of the Treaty of Rome called for the harmonisation of indirect taxation to ensure the proper functioning of the internal market. In 1967, two EC directives required the adoption of VAT by all Member States as a part of their tax systems. The United Kingdom joined the Community on the 1st of January

1973, and VAT was introduced in Britain for the first time three months later.

In May 1977, the EC passed its sixth VAT directive (77/3881EEC). This was a major step towards harmonisation. It laid down strict definitions of those goods which Member States could exempt, and required that VAT be levied on all other products. The United Kingdom was forced to end exemption and zero-rating in several areas by the European Court. Recently, a ruling on the 21st of June 1988 forced the United Kingdom to charge VAT on the construction of buildings, commercial fuel and power, sewerage and water supplied to industry, news services, and boots and helmets provided to employees.

Zero-rating restricted

Citing Article 99 of the Treaty of Rome, the Commission has worked devotedly to restrict zero-rating. The centralist ratchet is in full twist: Member States are free to end zero-rating on any items; but having done so, they are not allowed to reimpose it without the unanimous consent of the Council of Ministers.

The Commission has gone on to make it clear that the single market does not only require the harmonisation of VAT and excise duties, but also of direct taxes on business income.

On the 24th of June 1991, EC finance ministers agreed that Member States would apply a VAT rate of at least 15 per cent from the 1st of January 1993.

Reduced rates or zero-rating would be allowed on certain agreed items until 1996. Norman Lamont accepted the idea, and said that Britain would abide by the minimum standard rate of 15 per cent (Britain charges VAT at 17.5 per cent anyway). But he resisted the proposal that this should be a legal requirement, since conceding the principle that the EC should set British tax rates would constitute a massive loss of national sovereignty. However, he eventually agreed at a meeting on the 27th July 1992 that the decision should be made legally binding, but only for a limited period.

The importance of this decision should not be underestimated. It means that once VAT is charged on domestic fuel (or anything else for that matter) at a rate of over 15 per cent, it can never again be lowered or removed as a matter of EC law.

Fundamental problem

The issue of VAT demonstrates the fundamental problem with the structure of Community law, the *acquis communautaire*, which is like a vast magnet drawing political power irretrievably towards itself. Once a decision is made, for short-term domestic reasons, to transfer some areas of authority to the EC, that authority is lost forever to the nation. EC institutions thus preside over a self-driven and continuous accumulation of power. This is not a problem which derives from Maastricht although Maastricht exacerbates it by giving legal force to the extension of the *acquis communautaire*. Rather, it has its roots in the Treaty of Rome and the very foundations of the European Community.

If the Community is to succeed in adapting to the pressures of the future, it will have to re-examine its inherently inflexible and over-centralised legal constitution. If it fails to do so, it runs the risk of breaking apart in a welter of public fury as its peoples see their democratic rights steadily and irrevocably eroded.

11.

MAASTRICHT TREATY
INVALID

The entire ratification of the Maastricht Treaty depended on the German Constitutional Court decision given on 11th October 1993. There is now written confirmation from the British Government, the Bank of England and the Danish Central Bank that the German Court did NOT ratify the terms of the Treaty as signed at Maastricht. The Treaty therefore falls.

To fulfil the conditions for ratification of the Maastricht Treaty each individual member state had to ratify the Treaty. If one country failed then the whole treaty failed - that is why, notoriously, the Danes, having rejected the treaty, were asked to vote again.

Secondly it was not sufficient for each Government merely to say "yes, we approve the treaty". Article R of the Treaty requires that each country must ratify

"according to its own constitutional requirements"

In the German case the Government could only ratify if the Federal Constitutional Court (Bundes-verfassungsgericht) agreed that the terms of the treaty were in accord with their constitution (Grundgesetz). This they did not do.

In fact it is clear that the terms approved by the Court in Karlsruhe as constitutional **are not the terms of the actual treaty signed by the German Government**. The judges said for instance that;

"Article F of the Treaty does not empower the Union to procure the financial means or other means it deems necessary to fulfil its purposes."

But that is precisely what Article F does say:

"The Union shall provide itself with the resources necessary to attain its objectives and carry out its policies."

And following a question in the House of Lords, Baroness Chalker, Minister at the Foreign Office confirmed that the European Union

"can obtain financial resources to attain the Union's objectives."

Therefore both the terms of the Maastricht Treaty and the British Government flatly contradict the interpretation of the Treaty which led the German Court to permit ratification.

The German Court further asserted that Germany "has not subjected itself to an automatic movement towards monetary union beyond its control." In fact it has done just that, the terms of the treaty being quite clear:

"The high contracting parties declare the irreversible character of the Community's movement to the third stage of monetary union (ie a single currency) by signing the treaty provisions on Economic and Monetary Union."

Germany, unlike the United Kingdom and the Danish Government, did not exempt itself from this provision at Maastricht. (The German Court also ruled that Germany could leave the monetary union if the stability conditions were not continuously fulfilled. As the Governor of the Danish Central Bank recently wrote in the Financial Times "These reservations are more far reaching than Denmark's own exemption from EMU which gave rise to so much trouble")

The German interpretation of their obligations as regards a single currency have also been contradicted by the British Government. In reply to a question in the House of Lords,

Lord Henley for the Government (Written Answer 137, 10.2.94) confirmed that by 1 January 1999 at the latest

> "all member states judged by the Council to fulfil the necessary conditions for the adoption of a single currency will participate in stage 3" (ie a single currency)

In fact there will be no "judgment" required since the convergence criteria are already layed down and are very specific. The only way the Germans could decide NOT to fulfil the criteria would be to bring their economy to its knees and thereby fail to meet the criteria!

We have further contradiction of the German Court from the Bank of England. The Governor, in a letter to Rodney Atkinson, confirmed that although the United Kingdom

> "is under no obligation to move to the third stage of monetary union unless it notifies the European Union of its intention to do so. There is no equivalent provision in respect of the Federal Republic of Germany."

We therefore now have confirmation from the British Government, the Bank of England and the Danish Central Bank that the terms of the Maastricht Treaty as approved by the German Constitutional Court DO NOT EXIST. The Court merely approved a Treaty of its own imagination, in flat contradiction of the terms of the Treaty signed by the British, German and 10 other Governments at Maastricht.

Therefore the German Government did not in fact ratify the Treaty "according to its own constitutional requirements" as required by Article R and **therefore the entire ratification is invalid.**

It was of course extraordinary that the future of the United Kingdom and the powers of its Parliament should have been dependent firstly on two Danish referenda and secondly on German judges sitting in Karlsruhe. The German Court judgment was however critical to the whole ratification process and hence to British obligations under Maastricht and of course the Treaty of Rome itself.

The German Court judgment is so at variance with the terms of the treaty and the understanding of that treaty by authorities in Britain and Denmark that it is clear that both interpretations cannot be correct. It must be for individuals or corporations who cannot accept their obligations under the Maastricht Treaty to challenge ratification in the courts. They would seem to have an excellent chance of proving that, since ratification has not taken place, specific provisions of the treaty are unenforceable.

12.

GOVERNMENT A JUDGE
IN ITS OWN CAUSE

One of the most strict conventions of the democratic society established by the founding fathers of the United States of America was the division of powers between the Executive, the Legislature and the Judiciary.

In the United Kingdom such a formal distinction is less finely drawn and - as both the Maastricht Treaty and the recent arms to Iraq affair prove - there is a dangerous contamination of the legal process when the Attorney General, who heads the Crown Prosecution Service, is also the Government's senior law officer and a political appointee.

In the Arms to Iraq affair was it right for the Attorney General, a Government appointee, to have the power to attach public interest immunity certificates to documents needed by the defence in a case where the Government itself was implicated and where a Government department was bringing the case?

In the Maastricht treason charges we were confronted by the same problem. By presenting our case against the Treaty under the Misprision of Treason provisions of the Common Law, the case to be considered was a criminal case and the law officer responsible for the Crown Prosecution Service was, once again, the Attorney General, an appointee of the very institution we were (effectively) accusing of treason.

The first rule of natural justice is that no man may be a judge in his own cause "non judex in causa sua". It was on this matter that the following press release, in connection with the English cases and the following letter to the procurator fiscal in Lerwick, in connection with the accusations in the Scottish Courts, were issued by Norris McWhirter:

A breach of the first rule of natural justice has been alleged against the Attorney General, Sir Nicholas Lyell, for blocking examination of any of the seven charges of treason layed against the Foreign Secretary and the former MP Francis Maude for signing the Treaty of European Union at Maastricht on 7th February 1992.

The allegations are being made to the Lord Chancellor, who is the Cabinet Minister responsible for the adminsitration of justice. While the essence of the offence of treason lies in the violation of allegiance owed to the Sovereign, the seven "informations" originally layed against Messrs. Hurd and Maude make specific charges about the destruction of the British Constitution and the reduction of our Monarch to the status of a European citizen. Under the Treaty of Rome, as amended at Maastricht, the Queen can be arraigned in what were once her own courts, under superior European law. She is exposed, as are all European citizens, to another stream of personal taxation under Article 192 of the consolidated treaty.

Commenting on the impasse Norris McWhirter said: "Having denied the British electorate the opportunity of expressing any opinion about the Maastricht Treaty and giving its consent through referendum to the ending of British self governance,it is intolerable that Ministers of the Crown now seek to prevent any consideration by the judiciary as to whether what has been done is constitutional. Given that the Maastricht Treaty itself requires member countries to ratify it in accordance with their constitutional requirements, it is essential that our judiciary should be able to give its ruling on this matter.

Letter to Procurator Fiscal, Lerwick. 24th March 1994:

Your letter of 9th February states that you are directed by Crown Counsel to inform me that there is nothing laid before you which causes the Crown to alter its position ie to refuse to investigate the lawfulness of the destruction of Scotland's constitution in breach of a statute in force.

Accordingly, in the absence of any reasons whatsoever I do not regard my duty as discharged and reserve to myself the course of seeking to persuade privy counsellors to call for a reference to their Judicial Committee per the Judicial Committee Act 1833 s.4.

Unlike the civil case R versus Secretary of State for Foreign and Commonwealth Affairs, ex parte Rees Mogg of 30th July last, such process would be binding in Scotland and Northern Ireland.

The magisterial or procuratorial role in misprision, adopted into Scottish law in 1708, appears to be circumvented if Crown Counsel offers no reasons but only assertion that Scotland's constitution has not been destroyed, when in fact the ancient parliament of Great Britain has been clearly subjugated to a new overseas parliament, in which Scotland's members can be outvoted more than seven fold.

The law of natural justice, whereunder no man may be a judge in his own cause, appears to have been ignored insofar as Crown Counsels work under the superintendence of the Lord Advocate, adviser to Her Majesty's Government on precisely the constitutional propriety of the use of the prerogative power and on the constitutionality of the amendments to the European Communities Act.

13.

EUROPEAN SUPERSTATE
BACKED BY TORIES

The European People's Party (EPP), the centre-right umbrella group in the European Parliament which includes Tory MEPs, openly calls for the establishment of a federal European superstate.

Adopted by the ninth EPP Congress in Athens last November, the Basic Programme of the European People's Party calls for "the gradual - but resolute - transformation of the European Community into a genuine political union on a federal model ..." "A federal Europe," it goes on to state, "is now more than ever a necessary and realistic political objective."

As readers ponder these words and the further extracts from the EPP manifesto printed below, they should bear in mind that since Tory MEPs are officially part of the EPP group in the European Parliament, and since the EPP is allowed to have an office in Conservative Central Office, Government and Conservative assurances that the Maastricht Treaty marks a retreat from European federalism ring extremely hollow.

Extracts from the EPP manifesto:

211. The constitution of the Union will have to establish an effective mechanism and procedures for allocating powers not provided for when it entered into force. These new powers will be needed to ensure that the Union remains capable of adapting to new economic, social and technological challenges and to the needs of European development and the international political situation.

212. The Union must be given all the means necessary for the achievement of its objectives and the implementation of its policies. It will therefore be given a federal-type budget with sufficient resources managed on a 'progressive' basis, taking into account the relative prosperity of each Member State.

213. In this connection, the EPP is in favour of a direct relationship between the European Community and the taxpayer, thereby also giving the European Parliament direct responsibility vis-à-vis the taxpayer. (This is of course the essence of the loss of self government. With tax raising rights goes real political power.)

214. The EPP's institutional programme draws on the advances - and the gaps - in the Maastricht Treaty of 7 February 1992, which sanctioned the transition from the European Economic Community (EEC) to the European Community (EC) and to the European Union.

215. The Maastricht Treaty is an important step towards European Union. Its potential must be fully exploited and its shortcomings rectified.

218. The EPP will remain very vigilant and ensure that the intergovernmental action does not eventually take over from Community action (the exact opposite to John Major's "subsidiarity"). In particular it will ensure that the review of the Maastricht Treaty, which it hopes to see before 1996, will lead towards greater communitization and restore the unitary nature of the draft treaty adopted by the European Parliament (but rejected at Maastricht!).

Affirming federalism

219. The EPP strongly reaffirms the federative vision of the Christian Democrat pioneers of Europe. It stresses that the federal goal of European integration must be explicitly included in the Treaty on European Union.

224. It is clear, however, that in order to attain the already established objective of the internal market - the central axis of

the Single Act - the qualified majority vote has to apply to sectors formerly requiring unanimity (taxation, freedom of movement of persons, etc). This is even more true of the new objectives the Twelve set themselves in the Maastricht Treaty.

225. The progress of the Comununity towards a genuine European Union therefore implies above all an institutional system that is able to assume its responsibilities effectively.

226. First, that means meeting the new commitments entered into in the Maastricht Treaty, such as:

1. Increased protection for the rights of European citizens, common policies in fields such as immigration, right of asylum and help for refugees and effective combating of crossborder crime and terrorism at European level;

2. formulating a common foreign and security policy, eventually to include a common defence policy;

3. the creation of an Economic and Monetary Union on the basis of a single currency and an autonomous central bank, together with respect for the procedures and timetables set out to that end;

4. the obligation to tackle the new Community activities decided upon in the field of social policy, energy, civil protection and tourism;

5. the extension of the scale of Community powers in the fields of consumer protection, public health, research and development, industry trans-European networks (transport, telecommunications, energy) and the European dimension of culture and education.

An ominous threat

230. The Council procedure of unanimous voting must gradually be restricted (once again, the exact opposite of Major's "subsidiarity"). First of all, the field of application of the qualified majority vote must be extended to areas of prime

interest to the Community, such as important aspects of social and environmental policy,

231. The Commission is the motive force of the Community. As of now, its composition and powers will be more closely adapted to the needs of efficient management, taking account of the principle of subsidiarity and, above all, future enlargement. The EPP is therefore in favour of the emergence of a genuine European executive power, independent of the Council, which will hold legislative power together with the European Parliament and become a Chamber of Status (in other words a Government!).

233. The Court of Justice, which interprets and ensures observance of Community law, will have to be given the right to impose sanctions on Member States that do not respect its decrees (in fact fines on member states are included in the Maastricht Treaty).

253. The future constitution of the Union must also encompass areas of social policy which, in accordance with the subsidiarity principle, cannot be dealt with by the Member States alone. The implementation and extension of the Social Charter, which has been more or less blocked by the unanimity rule must be guaranteed.

14.

EURO-PARLIAMENT'S PLAN TO END THE NATION STATE

By a beguilingly cunning formula, those in the European Parliament intent on creating a European superstate, are seeking to make European federalism virtually unstoppable.

Article 47 of Title VII - Final Provision of the European Parliament's working document, the Constitution of the European Union, Doc. En/DT/234/234285 PE 203.601/B, reads:

> "The Constitution (of a future European Union) shall be considered adopted and shall come into force when it has been ratified by a majority of Member States representing four-fifths of the total population."

This formula means that the five least populous countries could not block the creation of a European State unless backed by a sixth nation with a population in excess of 64 and a half million - which could only be Germany.

The draft formula also ensures that the two most Euro-sceptical member nations - the United Kingdom (56 and a half million) and Denmark (5 and a quarter million) - would be 7 and a half million short of the number of votes needed to defend their right to self-determination by blocking the construction of such a Euro-State.

To cap it all, the Committee on Institutional Affairs in the European Parliament has issued the following breath-taking comment through its rapporteur, M. Fernand Herman:

"In calling for the adoption of a constitution which would progressively replace treaties (the Treaties of Rome and Maastricht and fifteen lesser treaties), the parliament is doing no more than adapting vocabulary to facts, and texts to reality.

"Such a Constitution would foster clarity and truth by putting an end to the fiction of the abiding intact sovereignty of the member states."

EACH one of our new 87 members of the European Parliament will cost the British tax-payer at least £919,000 - a total of £79.95 million a year to keep.

This includes: Personal Salaries £31,000 each; Secretarial and Office Allowance £92,484 each; Tax free expenses £40,000 per year; Attendance Allowance £155 per day. (See Appendix II for full costs of MEPs)

Costly new building

To add insult to injury, these MEPs have now acquired a grand new European Parliament building at the huge cost of £840 million, in which plenary sessions (as opposed to committee meetings etc.) will only take place 10 days a year!

In 1993, £3,810 million, Britain's net contribution, was syphoned off our Treasury to be spent by the Eurocrats of Brussels. For every £ extracted (gross) from the British taxpayer, 34.7p sticks to the Eurocrats and their redistributive programmes.

The British taxpayer is powerless to do anything about this, since not only are British ministers in a minority within the European Council, but in addition Britain's MEPs can be outvoted more than five and a half-fold by the fixed majority of 480 MEPs representing the other eleven EC 'partner' nations.

15.

FEDERALISM AND CONSERVATIVE MEPs

It is a characteristic of all politicians, when faced with the prospect of losing power, to say anything that they think their voters want to hear. Perhaps it is a characteristic we should expect. But for few politicians can the temptation be stronger than for the would-be MEP. With an average turnout of just over thirty per cent at European elections, he knows that he need only convince one out of every eight eligible voters to support him. Moreover, since few of his half-million constituents are aware of so much as his name, he can rest assured in the knowledge that his election rhetoric is extremely unlikely to be remembered or used against him. In any case, even if his constituents were interested in his performance, news of the European Parliament is notoriously hard to come by, and votes are often taken in secret. All in all, the MEP is quite justified in seeing elections as an infrequent irritant which should not be allowed to divert him from his main business of seeking to promote the Strasbourg Parliament as the basis of a federal European state.

Who can blame the Conservatives in the European Parliament for adopting, in accordance with this view, an anti-centralist tone for the June elections? They know that British voters have a stubborn allegiance to notions of national democracy and self- rule - so why not pander to these feelings? It will surely not be beyond Conservative candidates, representing a party traditionally associated with liberty and patriotism, to present themselves as less subordinated to Brussels than their opponents. After all, no-one has ever shown the slightest interest in MEPs' past policies or voting records; and no-one is likely to care what they do once they get re-elected. All that is needed, they reason, is a few months of stirring rhetoric about nation-states, freedom and decentralisation, just to see them through to the poll - once back in Strasbourg, they can return to their chief task: seeking to bring about the political and economic unification of Europe.

The EPP: Unashamed Federalists

One of the clearest examples of this new strategy was a flurry of letters to The Times at the end of last year in which Conservative Euro-MPs sought to distance themselves from the European People's Party, the extreme federalist Christian Democratic grouping in the European Parliament which the Conservatives joined enthusiastically in 1992. Sir Christopher Prout, leader of the Conservatives in the European Parliament, protested that they were only "allied members of the EPP Parliamentary Group," and, as though to emphasise the point, signed himself "Christopher Prout MEP (European People's Party Parliamentary Group (Conservative))," rather than "European People's Party (Conservative)" as he had always done until then.

One can quite understand why Sir Christopher is making this frantic, if belated, attempt to deny his links with the EPP, for the EPP has always prided itself on its federalist zeal and on its adherence to an interventionist "social market" ideology.

"The EPP shall pursue the process of federal unification and compete for the realization of a United States of Europe," proclaims the EPP Constitution.

The EPP's Basic Programme adopted in 1992, the drafting of which involved Conservative MEPs, is no less explicit.

> A federal Europe is now more than ever a necessary and realistic political objective.
>
> (paragraph 202)
>
> The EPP is in favour of a direct relationship between the European Community and the taxpayer, thereby also giving

89

the European Parliament direct responsibility vis-à-vis the taxpayer.

(paragraph 213)

Economic development... cannot really dispense well-being and act as a real factor of peace unless its fruits are equally distributed. That is why we must support and develop systems of collective solidarity.

(paragraph 138)

The recently published EPP manifesto for the June elections backs monetary union and the Social Chapter, and aims to "advance resolutely towards European unification".

While Conservative candidates will produce a domestic manifesto of their own (or rather have one forced upon them by Central Office strategists), this will have no bearing upon their obligation to uphold EPP policies. Nor will it have anything to do with their actual views. Appearing on ITV's Walden programme on 6th March 1994, Sir Edward Heath spelt out the kind of manifesto on which he felt that Tory candidates must stand if they were to be consistent in their principles, including full political union, the phasing out of the national veto and monetary union "as soon as possible". "I know many of the candidates personally", he said. "They want this manifesto as well".

"Fully Integrated with the EPP"

The sudden claim by the Conservatives in the European Parliament that they are not proper members of the EPP but only "allied members of the EPP Parliamentary Group" simply will not stand close scrutiny. The Constitution of the EPP is quite unequivocal: "The Christian Democratic parties of the member countries and their Group in the European Parliament make up the European People's Party." There is no distinction between being a member of the Parliamentary Group and being a member of the EPP.

Conservative MEPs were well aware of this when they joined. Their press statement at the time described them as "now fully integrated with the EPP," and the EPP has retained an office at Conservative Central Office ever since, just as at the headquarters of its other constituent political parties.

Indeed, the Conservatives' official publications described the EPP as "a party political organisation equipped to fight European elections on a trans-national basis with a common manifesto," (Conservatives in the European Parliament, 1992, p. 16).

The Conservatives in the European Parliament have taken wholeheartedly to the EPP's ideas and policies, delighting their fellow Christian Democrats with their enthusiasm for political union. When asked whether the Conservatives had agreed to abide in full by the EPP programme, an EPP spokesman replied: "We would not have accepted them if they had not... and they have more than lived up to their promises". (Jean Penders MEP, BBC On The Record, 24 October 1993.)

The Conservatives in the European Parliament have taken to explaining that they only linked up with the EPP as a way of "strengthening the influence and authority of the Centre-Right in the European Parliament." This claim is patently absurd. If Tory MEPs wanted to bolster the anti-socialist vote, they simply had to continue to vote that way. The Gaullists sit detached from the EPP as part of the European Democratic Alliance which comprises the French RPR, half-a-dozen Irish Fianna Fail, two Spaniards and a Greek. No-one accuses them of undermining the Centre-Right, and they seem to feel no urgent need to join the EPP. The claim that joining the EPP has brought Conservative Euro-MPs friends and influence is equally ill-founded. In the January vote of confidence in Lord Owen, for example, EPP deputies from France, Germany, Holland and Italy were in the forefront of what was widely seen as an anti-British motion; Tory MEPs were supported only by their compatriots in the British Labour Party.

The Conservatives' link with the EPP should be recognised for what it is - a full-blown union among like-minded politicians who share the aspiration of building a federal European state with the Commission as its executive government, the European Court as its supreme court, the European Parliament as its main legislature and the European Council as a sort of *Bundesrat* or Upper House representing the provinces (i.e. the Member States). If there is any doubt as to the enthusiasm with which Conservative MEPs embrace the integrationist and centralist policies of the rest of the EPP, it should be dispelled by the following policy statements.

In their own words

ON FEDERALISM:

"[The European Parliament" calls for a move from the present Community based on the Treaties to a Union of the federal type on a constitutional basis."

(This phrase appears in several resolutions supported and voted for by Conservative MEPs between 14 February 1984 and last year.)

"underlines its grave concern at the emergence of some positions within the Council defining political union' as merely a reinforcement of the intergovernmental level of co-operation among the governments of the EC".

(Resolution by the European Parliament, 11 July 1990, supported and voted for by Conservative MEPs.)

"considers that the requirement for unanimity for ordinary Community legislation is tantamount to the dictatorship of the minority".

(ibid.)

ON ECONOMIC AND MONETARY UNION:

"It is vital that we rejoin [the ERM] as soon as possible. We do not want to find ourselves in the second division".

(John Stevens MEP, At The Heart Of Europe, Conservatives in the European Parliament, 1993.)

"We have secured our right to choose; but we should be mad to choose anything less than first class".

(Ben Patterson MEP, European Monetary Union, Conservatives in the European Parliament).

"We in Britain need monetary union more than most... we cannot go back to the floating pound which cost us so much money."

(Sir Fred Catherwood MEP, At The Heart Of Europe, op. cit.)

ON SUBSIDIARITY:

Conservative MEPs have made clear that they would like to see strict limits to the areas covered by subsidiarity.

"[The European Parliament] advocates respect for the 'acquis communautaire' [i.e. the occupied field' theory which states that EC authority is irreversibly entrenched in any area in which it has once acted], and holds the view that the division of tasks, spheres of activity and competences must make allowance for the stage reached at present, as well as the inevitable evolving of the Union".

(Resolution on the Principle of Subsidiarity, 12 July 1990, supported and voted for by Conservative MEPs.)

"considers it indispensible for a European Union on a federal model to possess the competences already entrusted to the European Community and the competences essential, in particular, for the achievement of economic and monetary union, common foreign and security policies and the establishment of a People's Europe".

(ibid.)

When, following the Edinburgh summit, the European Commission made a token gesture towards subsidiarity by withdrawing some health and safety and environmental regulations, Tory MEPs were loud in their condemnation.

"I cannot believe that the Commission or the European Parliament would wish to see this legislation scrapped in the name of subsidiarity".

(Richard Simmons MEP, At The Heart Of Europe, op. cit.)

"The Commission is seeing what else it can jettison. We have a fight on our hands. Some of the battles we thought we had won we'll have to win again."

(Caroline Jackson MEP, ibid.)

"I would rather have gremlins in blue uniforms - with twelve gold stars - ensuring that we have safe food than have gremlins in the food itself".

(Caroline Jackson MEP, ibid.)

ON SOCIAL POLICY:

"Conservatives support a social dimension to the Single Market". (50 Questions And Answers On The European Community, Conservatives in the European Parliament, 1992.

"[The European Parliament]" considers that the objectives of social policy, as defined in the treaties, should be extended, improved and completed, notably by...adding that the completion and further evolution of the internal market necessarily imply provisions to secure the convergence, at higher levels of living and working conditions".

(Resolution by the European Parliarnent, 11 July 1990, supported and voted for by Conservatives in the European Parliament.)

ON AGRICULTURE:

"The CAP has been too successful".

(50 Questions And Answers On The European Community, op.cit.)

ON FOREIGN POLICY:

"[The European Parliament] calls for the Council (rather than a separate framework of foreign ministers) to be given the prime responsibility for defining [foreign] policy; for the Commission to have a right of initiative in proposing policies to the Council and to have a role in representing the Community externally; and for the Communtiy's foreign policy to be subject to scrutiny by the Comunity's elected Parliament".

(Resolution of ll July 1990, op cit.)

"considers that membership of international organisations should be adjusted accordingly, with the Community as such representing the Member States in those areas where the Community's competence has been established".

(ibid.)

The views and policies of the Conservatives in the European Parliament are clearly incompatible, not only with basic Conservative principles, but even with the relatively integrationist programme of John Major's pro-Maastricht administration. Where Mr Major has condemned federalism and described plans for monetary union as being "about as relevant as a rain dance," the MEPs who supposedly represent his party are falling over each other in their haste to bring about full political and economic union. Their views are unlikely to strike a chord with voters who lost homes or jobs during the disastrous experience of ERM membership, and who have no desire to switch their allegiance to a foreign political authority. As the true nature of the Conservative MEPs' agenda is understood, they are likely to pay a heavy electoral price.

16.

THE EUROPEAN PARLIAMENT: A NEGATION OF DEMOCRACY

Democracy and national sovereignty are the same thing.

Charles de Gaulle

Direct elections to the European Assembly are not an extension of parliamentary self-government; they are a negation of parliamentary self-government.

Enoch Powell

The Next Battlefield

The existing structure of the European Community presents its advocates with something of a PR problem and they know it. The Commission's sole right to initiate policy leaves the driving force of the EC in the hands of unelected officials, politicians sent to Brussels after a poor performance at home who, once there, are wholly unanswerable for their actions. Since any increase in the authority of the EC means shifting powers from elected representatives to these unaccountable bureaucrats, the opponents of closer European integration have always becn able to argue that the power of the EC can only grow at the expense of democratic accountability. Stung by this criticism, the Euro-federalists were not long in formulating their solution: an increase in the powers of the European Parliament.

The smaller nations of the EC have always supported the elevation of the Strasbourg Parliament as the basis of a federal Europe, seeing federalism as the way to safeguard their interests against more powerful states. Belgian and Dutch diplomats, in particular, tend to follow the paths trodden out by their respective post-war foreign ministers, Paul-Henri Spaak and Joseph Luns, who saw federal structures as their guarantee against Franco-German hegemony. Only recently, however, have the larger states come to support the notion. Pro-Europeans in France see democratic federalism as the answer to the fears of an unaccountable bureaucracy which surfaced during their Maastricht referendum, while Germans are bound by the decision of their Constitutional Court, which ruled on October 12th 1993 that an increase in the powers of the European Parliament was a precondition for further European integration.[1]

The role of the European Parliament is likely to be one of the most fiercely contested issues between now and the 1996 Intergovernmental Conference. Proposals to elevate its position raise critical questions about the nature of democracy and the pretensions of the EC toward statehood or even nationhood. Can parliamentary democracy be made to work in a state comprising 340 million citizens, thirty languages and dialects and well over a hundred major political parties? Can we foresee transnational party spokesmen husting in different languages up and down Europe, selling a common manifesto? More importantly, can we see voters transferring their allegiance to a European legislature and tuning in to watch those hustings? It is over these questions that the next battle for European integration will be fought.

From Messina to Maastricht

The debate about the powers of the European Parliament derives from an ambiguity over its role which has always been present in the EC. To the pragmatists, to Britain and her allies, the European Assembly (as it originally was) was a body not unlike a shareholders' committee, whose function was to scrutinise the Commission. To the federalists, however, and to the MEPs themselves, the European Parliament (as they took to calling it) was the body which would eventually form the legislature of the United States of Europe. In pursuit of this vision, MEPs ignored their intended function of controlling the Commission in order to give themselves the role, the status and all the trappings of a national parliament. Between 1958 and 1960 they worked out plans for being directly elected - plans which the Member States, for various reasons, chose to ignore. In 1969, the European Parliament threatened to go to the European Court if its proposals went disregarded. In effect, however, it had no means to push through its plans: the only power which it had was that of rejecting parts of the EC budget, and the MEPs, being dedicated federalists, would not risk slowing the pace of integration by exercising this power. In 1974, the Council decided in principle to allow direct elections. There was some opposition from Britain and Denmark, as well as from French Gaullists - although the latter were mollified when the French Constitutional Court declared that direct elections in themselves, without an increase in the powers of the European Parliament, constituted no threat to national sovereignty. British opposition continued until Callaghan was forced to concede direct elections as the price for continued Liberal support at home.

Direct elections altered the nature of the European Parliament fundamentally. Bolstered by their new legitimacy, MEPs wasted no time in setting about their self-appointed agenda of turning Strasbourg into a proper federal parliament. Instead of 198 part-time delegates from the Member States, there were now 410 full-time (in theory at least) elected representatives. Proper parliamentary procedures were drawn up, with debates, political groups and committees modelled on continental national parliaments. In 1981, it became customary for the head of government serving as President of the Community to appear before the European Parliament to deliver a "State of the Union Address", as though he were a national executive president reporting to his parliament. In 1984, the European Parliament formulated its draft proposals on European Union, which demanded a role for itself in economic and monetary union, in a common foreign policy and in the development of a European citizenship (all new ideas at that time) as well as a legislative role. Undeterred by a reduced turnout at that year's European elections, MEPs, including the British Conservatives, have continued to advocate the 1984 draft, using it as the basis of their demands at Maastricht and since.

The proposals call for an end to the so-called "democratic deficit". By this, the European Parliament means an end to the process by which powers formerly exercised by national parliaments pass to the "unelected" Council of Ministers (which it sees as insufficiently European in its outlook). That is to say, the European Parliament is not in any sense seeking to gain powers from the genuinely unaccountable parts of the EC, the Commission and the European Court. Rather, it wishes to extend its authority at the expense of properly democratic bodies: national parliaments and the ministers responsible to them. "Filling the democratic deficit" is thus an extremely misleading phrase. The powers of the Commission bureaucracy would continue to grow undisturbed; but authority would shift from national parliaments, whose legitimacy is recognised by their electorates, to Strasbourg. In May 1992, the European Parliament declared that it would veto the entry of any state wishing to join the EC unless it got its way on this issue.

The European Parliament After Maastricht

The European Parliament made three specific demands at Maastricht. First, the right to initiate legislation. Secondly, a system of co-decision which would place it on an equal footing with the Council. Thirdly, more powers to nominate the Commission. While none of these demands was granted in full, substantial concessions were made toward each of them. The right to initiate legislation was half granted: Article 137A allows the Parliament to request the Commission to submit any appropriate proposal. Co-decision with the Council was likewise only partially granted, for the scales remain tipped in favour of the Council which may act independently if agreement cannot be reached within six weeks (unless an absolute majority of MEPs objects within a further six weeks). As regards the Commission, the European Parliament wanted a role in electing the President, a vote of confidence in the new Commission and a synchronisation of Commission and Parliamentary terms of office. Here it got its way, except that its contribution to the appointment of the President is only consultative.

A New Constitution

The European Parliament has long been ardent in its advocacy of a federal state. It envisages the Commission as the executive branch of the new federal government, a sort of European cabinet. The European Parliament itself would constitute the main legislative body, elected on a common franchise, while the Council would become a sort of Upper House or *Bundesrat* representing the Member States. The European Court of Justice would become the supreme court.[2]

Thus, the European Parliament has not entirely abandoned its role of controlling the Commission, but it now seeks to do so as a parliament monitoring its executive ministers on the Continental model. Hence its demand to nominate the President following its own election: the executive would emerge as the popular choice of an elected legislature as in most European states. The original notion, that the Strasbourg Assembly was a way for the Member States to scrutinise the worst excesses of EC bureaucracy, has long been forgotten.

A new federal state on this model, argues the Parliament, would overcome the problem of the lack of democratic accountability inherent in the EC's current structure. A federal constitution would define those areas of policy to be decided at European level, including the EC's present "competences", foreign and security policy, economic and monetary policy and citizenship rights.[3] In each of these areas, the European Parliament would uphold the democratic will of the people of Europe.

This blueprint relies on the assumption that the peoples of Europe will be content to entrust the protection of their rights to a supranational parliament, that they will be prepared to accept the legitimacy of representatives elected by foreigners. This is an assumption which must be tested.

Competent to Govern?

On one level, proposals to elevate the Strasbourg Parliament run up against the all too evident mediocrity of the body itself. Few would deny, for example, that the rate of attendance is extremely poor. It is rare to find as many as a hundred of the 518 MEPs at any given session, whatever the importance of the debate. A number of Euro-MPs have turned up only once or twice in the last year; some have failed to attend at all. When MEPs do bother to vote on policy, that policy often turns out to be wildly quixotic or straightforwardly buffoonish. At the end of 1993, the European Parliament commissioned a detailed study of the phenomenon of UFOs (which reached the astounding conclusion that UFOs might exist, but might not). At around the same time, the Parliament decided to allocate £336,000 of EC funds earmarked for the promotion of democracy in Russia to Ruslan Khasbulatov, just days before he launched his Communist insurrection. More recently, it has emerged that certain MEPs are in contact with Gerry Adams with the aim of inviting him to address the Parliament. Against this rather *opera bouffe* background, it has been calculated that each MEP costs the taxpayer £919,961, including tax-free expenses and a generous attendance allowance - that is,more than three times as much as a Westminster MP.

Yet MEPs are elected on a derisory turnout, which has declined in every European election since 1979. In Britain, only thirty-five per cent of those eligible to vote in the last European election did so. That is to say, sixty-five per cent of electors failed to vote for the candidate who claims to be their democratic representative. The overwhelming majority of constituents are not even aware of their Member's name.

Anyone who has observed the Strasbourg Parliament in action will have been struck by the Walter Mittyish comicality of deputies who are unknown by their constituents and who rarely bother to involve themselves in the daily grind of politics, earnestly debating the great issues facing Europe and voting to award themselves enormous new powers. In truth, the European Parliament's vast appetite for new powers is matched only by its Members' lack of interest in the powers which it currently exercises.

Europe - Votre Patrie

This is not, of course, an argument in principle against increasing the power of the European Parliament. For it could be argued that the low level of public interest in the Parliament and the low calibre of its Members are symptoms of its lack of importance. Upgrade its status and the problem will disappear.

We are therefore forced back to the key question of whether the peoples of Europe will recognise the legitimacy of a European body of this kind, whether they will owe it allegiance, accept its policies and obey its laws.

The defining feature of a successful democracy is that each citizen feels sufficient community of interest with his fellow electors to accept their majority decisions and abide by the laws made by their representatives. Indeed it is possible to go further and say that this willingness to live under common laws and institutions is the true test of nationhood. Certainly other factors such as language, culture and history may contribute to this sense. But ultimately, a state will hold together because its citizens accept government from each other. Germany and Italy came together as states in the Nineteenth Century because their peoples felt that they had enough in common one with another to accept a common government. Where this sense has been absent, such as in Austria-Hungary, Yugoslavia or the Soviet Union, political unity has been rejected, often with armed force.

In order, then, for a powerful European Parliament to be successful, the peoples of the Member States would have to feel some sense of European identity. Only if they see themselves primarily as Europeans will the people of, for example, Britain be prepared to abide by majority decisions of French, Dutch and Greek voters with which they disagree. British MEPs constitute fifteen per cent of the Strasbourg Parliament. Even if they and their constituents are unanimous on a policy issue, they may be overruled. Unless the British feel an overriding sense of loyalty as European citizens, they will react with angry and hostile nationalism whenever an unpopular or damaging policy is forced upon them.

Will this sense of European identity develop in Britain and the rest of the Community? All the evidence indicates that only a small minority of EC nationals see themselves as European in any significant sense. More importantly, opinion polls suggest that their number has fallen sharply since 1991.[4] The explanation for this decline is simple: experience of the practice of common European policies (in this case most obviously the ERM) has led to an anti-Brussels backlash as people see their needs being sacrificed to wider European interests. The last two years have been a mild demonstration of the nationalism and xenophobia which results from peoples being forced against their will to live under common laws and policies - a nationalism which will become increasingly fierce as the Maastricht process is pursued, as people lose their jobs because their domestic needs are subsumed into a European policy.

Herein, ultimately, lies the folly of increasing the powers of the European Parliament. Parliamentary democracy on a European scale will not work without a sense of European identity. Such a sense is felt by a small and shrinking minority of Europeans; and the enforcement of a powerful European legislature without (or at least before) the development of a European identity will have the effect of retarding rather than boosting such a development.

The Democratic Alternative

Support for the development of a federal Europe governed by a democratic European Parliament relies on the assumption that Europeans would feel a strong sense of loyalty to a European government - a view borne out neither by opinion testing nor by history. The intergovernmentalist position relies upon the converse view: that people see their own institutions as peculiarly legitimate, that they are happy to accept government from their compatriots as they are not from others.

According to this view, it is not the European Parliament but the Council of Ministers which has the true democratic mandate, accountable as it is to national governments whose legitimacy is recognised by their electors. If the balance of power among the EC Institutions is to be restructured, reform should be aimed at restoring the Community to a properly democratic base. This means stripping the Commission and the European Court of their much abused law-making powers and increasing the authority of the Council as a mechanism for effective intergovernmental unity.

It must be recognised that the European Parliament will never have proper democratic legitimacy. Public interest in the body, judged by turnout figures at European elections, has declined sharply from an already low base in 1979[5]. Elections are fought in every country on a domestic agenda; there is no evidence that voters are influenced by wider European questions. Despite procedural requirements which encourage parties to join together in transnational political groups, the eighty parties represented in the European Parliament have largely independent agendas of their own.

The time has come to do away with the pretence that accountable democracy can flourish at European level. Instead, efforts should be made to strengthen co-operation among the parliaments as well as the governments of the Member States. Radical reform of the EC Institutions is long overdue. As part of a wide reform aimed at putting the Community along a democratic intergovernmental path, the entire concept of an elected European Parliament should be dropped. Inasmuch as there is a need to keep checks upon the bureaucracy, this role should be performed by an Assembly composed of parliamentarians from the Member States.

Delegates to such an Assembly would enjoy greatly enhanced democratic legitimacy, being elected on a serious turnout and representing national parliaments with a recognised role. They would, moreover, act as a focus for interparliamentary co-operation among the Member States. It is important that, if inter- governmentalisrn is to be built up as a serious alternative to federalism, collaboration among national legislatures should complement the partnership of the executives.

The European Parliament should be recognised as an experiment which failed. Only if it is swept aside will the way be clear for real democracy in Europe.

NOTES:

[1] "Democratic legitimation is conveyed by the European Parliament elected by the people... the democratic basis of union should keep pace with integration" Karlsruhe Court decision, 12th October, 1993

[2] Draft Report on the Constitution of the European Union DOC EN/PR/234/234101 PE 203.601/rev 9th September, 1993

[3] Ibid.

[4] Survey by the Henley Centre of 7,000 EC nationals, 1993; also Eurobarometer polls

[5] From 62.8% to 58.4%

17.

AMERICAN FEDERALISM AND EUROPEAN NATIONS

When the American federalists fashioned the Constitution of the United States of America they were conscious of their emergence as ONE NATION from the struggles with the former colonial power. The "revolutionary war" was much more a war for aspirant nationhood than a revolution. Nevertheless, uppermost in the minds of the founders were the Christian and libertarian notions of a society for individuals and families free from the absolute power of the state.

The American fathers of the Constitution were the inheritors of the English principles of the rights of man and the wisdom of the Common Law - as opposed to the detailed constitution and state interventions common in European politics. But above all they were conscious of their identity as one nation. In his book "Conservatism in Danger" (1991) Rodney Atkinson described the vital differences between the organic structures of a Conservative Society. He contrasted them with the inorganic, politicised structures of a socialist society. In the former the nation is perhaps the organic entity of the greatest power and influence to which man has freely given his allegiance. And it was the consciousness of their one nation, with one language and one religion, free from foreign domination that inspired and informed the American constitution. Needless to say this is not, nor conceivably ever could be, the situation in a European Union of 12 nations and 9 languages.

The Americans of the late 18th century (beneficiaries of what they saw as the intellectual fruits of the Enlightenment) layed down the principles of individual freedom, personal property, religious freedom, a government system based on a division of countervailing powers and a people governed less by political majorities and more by (few) laws based on universal principles. What a contrast to even the embryo "Union" created in Europe with its overriding powers, social interventions and economic controls.

In the USA it was "federalism" which seemed to provide this structure. If the individual states delegated only those powers to federal government which the latter strictly needed for the general emancipation of the nation and if the rights of the individual were well defined and written into the constitution then the necessary dynamic and countervailing forces of a free society would exist.

Such a degree of integration, co-operation and legal unity could not reasonably be applied in an international federation like that of the European Union. But in fact the reverse has become the case with many British MPs rightly claiming that the individual American states still have more power than the nations of the European Union. There are widely differing income and sales taxes in the city, state and federal jurisdictions in the USA while the European Union already lays down minimum VAT rates, levels of national debt, inflation and government spending.

While the American states' rights are still substantial and offer competing centres of power to Washington, the European Commission already initiates laws for individual national governments, whose parliaments (following various treaties and in the UK the 1972 European Communities Act) can do no more than rubber stamp those laws. Indeed many directives and regulations from Brussels do not come before national parliaments at all.

While the American states' laws are sacrosanct, the European Court makes new law, not according to an agreed constitution but in accordance with its self proclaimed mission to "overcome national barriers to European integration". The European Court regularly suspends the laws of member states, and not on matters upholding the rights of individuals, but, as with the British "Merchant Shipping Act" actually depriving a member state of its property (internationally recognised fishing stocks).

James Madison, one of the fathers of the American constitution, noted that

> "The smaller the number of individuals composing a majority....the more easily will they concert and execute their plans of oppression."

How truly is that danger present in the decision making of the 12 Council of Ministers, making policy for over 300m people in the European Union, only 35% of whom vote in "European" elections.

One of the main reasons given for the federal principle was the promotion of free trade - or rather the prohibition by federal government of protectionist measures by individual states. This was of course also the excuse for the initial stages of the European Union, called the "Common Market". Needless to say neither group of politicians really intended their projects to be non political free trade areas to promote the interests and freedoms of the people. Rather they intended to promote the power interests of politicians, federal centralised power, ever greater interventions in the lives of individuals and states and the subsequent projection of that power overseas.

The irrelevance of the individual for such plans is best demonstrated in the democratic sounding principle of "freedom of movement of people" common to the "Unions" on both sides of the Atlantic. At first glance this looks like a basic individual freedom providing economic opportunity and an escape from potential political tyranny. But freedom of movement is principally an economic freedom of countries and corporations to direct labour to where its use will be most profitable. It is instructive to note that the first to descend in large numbers on Brussels office blocks and restaurants were not the democratic representatives of the people but highly payed corporate lobbyists. And the first to descend on Washington after the civil war were the displaced blacks from the southern states, dependent to this day on state welfare and the drug trade! For the great mass of people in America and Europe freedom of movement is an alienating, exhausting burden, and often a last resort for those who must choose between poverty and family break up.

Similarly the right of individuals to appeal over the heads of the American states or European nations directly to federal institutions sounds like an opportunity rather than a threat. But it is quite clear that federal powers have seen such individual rights (and the rights of regions within states) as a way of marginalising and eventually extinguishing the very entities to which individuals, families and communities feel most loyal. Even today a Californian feels distinct from a Texan and a Texan hardly feels at home in New York. In Europe the linguistic and cultural homes of individuals in nations make the attempts of the federal powers to bypass national governments by appealing to individual "rights" even more suspect and far less acceptable.

Even though the US constitution was based on "individual sovereignty" the individual was seen to have concluded a "social contract" with states and federal government and that contract could only be delivered if those institutions in turn enjoyed their sovereign identity and rights. Of course the people as a whole could withdraw their support. How different from the scandalous betrayal of popular sovereignty in the United Kingdom when the people were not consulted about the destruction of their constitution at Maastricht. And whereas it is an established practice in constitutional democratic states that significant internal statutes, never mind sovereign powers, cannot be overturned without 2/3 majorities in one or both houses, in not one referendum held in Europe on the Maastricht Treaty did any nation give anything like 2/3 approval. In France the majority was 51% to 49% while in Denmark it was 53% to 47% and in Sweden 52% to 48%

although in all three countries "pro union" governments oustspent their opponents by factors of up to 20 times!

Article 1 section 8 of the US constitution gave the US congress in Washington the power to regulate national (ie inter-state) trade and commerce. This was designed - as were the trade tasks of the European Commission - to prevent dumping, unfair subsidies and state manipulation of trade. In Felix Morley "Freedom and Federalism" Liberty Press 1981, page 6 the relevant article is described as reflecting

> "an original judgement that nationalizing the governance of commerce would help protect property and economic liberties from the oppressive tendencies of state legislatures."

This has certanly not been the effect of the European Community's central powers. For whereas the Commission in Brussels, acting as a kind of "office of fair trading" seeks to prevent massive state subsidy of steel, car, computer and airline businesses in Italy, France, Spain and Belgium, their proposals were simply outvoted by the pseudo "federal authority" - the Council of Ministers.

In other words the very principle defined by Madison in the USA and Howe and Hurd in Britain - that "majority voting prevents state tyranny" and would aid free trade, has been turned on its head. Majority voting guarantees nothing. Indeed it turns matters of universal principle into the plaything of political voting and opportunist trade off.

Similarly the most basic principle of a free society - personal property rights - has been totally undermined both by the British government and by the European ("federal") Court of Justice. When the "Leasehold Reform" legislation in the United Kingdom allowed leaseholders of property to force freeholders to sell, this obviously conflicted with the most basic right in a democratic society - to own private property. The Duke of Westminster - a substantial freeholder of residential property in central London - took his case against this illiberal and retrospective legislation to the European Court of Justice (sic) where it was dismissed. So much for the federal protection of the liberty of the individual.

The American constitution "reserved to the states all legitimate powers of government that were not explicitly delegated to the federal government". How different from the practice of "acquis communautaire" in Europe. Where (without the constraints of a constitution) the EU legislates in a particular field then that field becomes the exclusive responsibility of the Union and thereby deprives the nations of those rights for ever. This principle alone completely negated the "subsidiarity" clause in the Maastricht Treaty (the European equivalent of the Tenth Amendment).

Even in the USA the powers protecting individual rights (Ninth Amendment) and those protecting states' rights (Tenth) have been modified, ignored and overruled as the central federal power has grown. As Bolick notes (European Federalism: Lessons from America, Institute of Economic Affairs, London 1994)

> "Indeed the Ninth Amendment has never, in all of American history, provided the basis for Supreme Court invalidation of government actions; hence the sobriquet "the Forgotten Ninth.""

Indeed it was to override private property rights (in slave ownership) that federal authority engaged in a civil war and appropriated more powers to suppress the states' autonomy. It was only after the civil war that the 14th Amendment declared protection for both freedom and property - a complete contradiction while slavery existed but not so afterwards. But the slavery issue could have been resolved (unlike the enforceability of the Union) by the federal government simply buying out the slave owners - who had entered into perfectly legal contracts when slavery was legal.

There has never been any real discussion in the nearly 40 years history of the European Community of the rights of individuals. In a sense this is not surprising since even the most naive and ignorant national politician probably instinctively realised that such "federally" determined rights were a threat to his own control over "his" own nationals.

For although most would accept the constraints of universal declarations of the UN or the European Court of Human Rights (NO connection with the European Community and its own "Court of Justice") they would also accept that their notions of most individual and social rights were so intimately connected with their own nation's world view, culture and history that they would be better reflected and enshrined by national rather than supranational government.

Perhaps the most fundamental comparison between the European Union today and the early years of the American Union is in the right to secession. There is no such right in the various European Treaties and it was Lincoln's claim that there was no such right in the American Union Treaty which was the prime cause of the American civil war in 1861 (resulting in 364,511 deaths). But in 1828 a more interesting - and for the European Union an equally significant cause of friction - arose. Congress enacted substantial import tariffs to which the states objected. Bolick quotes the lawyer John Calhoun for the states' rights.

> "To maintain the ascendancy of the constitution over the lawmaking majority is the great and essential point on which the success of the American system must depend: unless that ascendancy can be preserved the necessary consequence must be that the laws will supersede the Constitution and finally *the will of the Executive, by the influence of its patronage, will supersede the laws...*"
> (authors' emphasis)

This is precisely what happened to the constitution of the United Kingdom on the basis of legislation instigated in "Europe" and enacted in UK laws between 1972 and 1992. So many basic statutes of the British Constitution (dating back to the 13th century) have been overturned by various international treaties on Europe that the British people and their ancient and famous parliament now effectively have a far more recent "constitution" than Germany - whose own 1949 constitution the British helped to write! Age did not weary the British constitution nor did the years condemn - it was condemned and destroyed by Brussels and a combination of ignorance and deceit at Westminster.

Calhoun also refers to how the executive's patronage "will supersede the laws". The arrogant assertion of such patronage was very recently demonstrated as the British Government forced through Parliament (as part of its annual Finance Bill) a substantial additional payment to the European Union budget. Ministers claimed, even before the debate, that an international treaty agreement to donate these funds made it inconceivable that they would tolerate a defeat. This was despite the absence of a manifesto commitment. In addition, no separate parliamentary bill had been presented prior to ministers signing the Edinburgh agreement - under "Crown Prerogative"!

When a number of its own MPs voted against the payment of hundreds of millions of pounds to a foreign institution where endemic fraud amounts to some £6,000m per annum the party whip was withdrawn. This contrasted with the relaxed treatment of MPs when, a week later, the major plank of the domestic budget was thrown out (Value Added Tax on domestic fuel bills). Already the budgetary requirements of the alien federal authority apparently take precedence over British self governance.

In 1828 in America the Congress backed down in the face of states' resistance and the import tariffs were modified. Within the EU today the protectionist moves come partly from the Union itself (see the struggle to approve GATT) and partly from the individual states who (especially France, Italy and Spain) continue state subsidies of various industries. When the USA retaliated against European steel subsidies, ALL EU states were hit, regardless of their individual innocence.

Of course federal authorities require new sources of income, separate from the states/nations, in order to finance their ambitions to become a fully fledged power. Import tariffs are an excellent source of such income (appealing as they do to xenophobic consumers and incompetent producers alike) as both the American and European Unions demonstrate. The European Union finances 23% of its entire budget with import levies. Some member states and the European Commission are urging an energy tax (in particular on oil in which the United Kingdom is very wealthy) ostensibly as an energy saving measure but in fact it is probably intended as an import control. Naturally it is not seen this way by the only substantial oil exporter - the United Kingdom - which finds itself in a similar position to the American states which resisted the 1828 import tariffs.

In The European Union, any such energy tax would of course benefit the overall union import bill. It would also benefit the very governments which, through state subsidy and ownership of energy utilities, force down energy prices and waste energy!

The "social Chapter" of the Maastricht Treaty on economic and monetary union seeks to impose detailed social and economic controls on companies, individuals and states. The UK has an "opt out" from this legislation although this has not prevented the EU imposing, by various dubious means, work place directives under "health and safety regulations". Although it was precisely such detailed socio-economic interventions in states which American federalism was designed to prevent, history, federal government and politicised supreme courts have conspired to overturn that principle. When the judiciary tried to act in the 1930s against Roosevelt's many federal interventions in industrial and labour markets the President threatened to change the Supreme Court's ideological balance. The Court backed down. (see Bolick page 36). By 1941 Federal government was even setting minimum wages and maximum working hours. It took the USA 170 years to become so interventionist. The European Union has started already!

This political arm-twisting of the "independent" judiciary is reminiscent of Chancellor Kohl's bullying of the "Bundesbank" in federal (West) Germany on reunification with the East. The most strict and successful monetary authority in Europe was pressured by the political authority into agreeing an irresponsibly high exchange rate between the West German and East German Marks. High inflation (itself a breaker of contracts and an illegal method of tax raising) ensued in the West and much higher unemployment than necessary in the East.

The political overrides the monetary. The federal centre overrides the constituent states. The majority overrides the constitution. Opportunity overrides principle. "Urgent" political aims override the operation of more gradual legal principles. In all these processes the state grows in power as the individual loses his freedom.

But the states or nations rights are no safer than individuals' rights. The Major government in the United Kingdom took comfort from the so-called "subsidiarity" clause in the Maastricht Treaty whereby in theory only that which can best be done by the centre will be taken from the member states. The American 10th Amendment reserved to the states all powers not expressly delegated to the federal government. But the Supreme Court declared (Bolick page 37):

> "the amendment states but a truism that all is retained which is not surrendered. There is nothing in the history of its adaptation to suggest that it was more than declaratory of the relationship between the national and state governments."

So much for federal government as a libertarian check on central power. A fundamental pillar of American federalism becomes no more than a "truism". Neither the American nor the European versions of "subsidiarity" are of any value. Bolick page 39:

> "...the record of American federalism on protecting individual liberty, securing an inviolable sphere for state

government autonomy and limiting the powers of federal government is poor."

Indeed as soon as treaty agreements permit the emergence of a new legal system relevant to more than one state or nation then the game is up. Eight years before the United Kingdom entered the European "Common Market", the 1964 ruling of the European Court of Justice in the Coster v ENEL case spoke of the fateful "transfer of domestic legal systems into the Community legal system".

Once a supreme logic, never mind power, has been established for limited application, day to day pragmatism, "emergency" intervention, political opportunism, case law creativity and blatant power building will extend the tentacles of the new power into every area of state, regional and individual life. Those who understood the limits of what could be done supranationally end up fighting the results of the political fantasies of those who understood nothing. Bolick, an American observer of the tragic events in the United Kingdom pinpoints the irony:

> "that those most sceptical of European federalism were often the greatest proponents of a federal Europe's purported objectives - free trade and strong defence."

These were of course also the prime aims behind the American Union - at first. But the lesson of American federalism, far from being an example, is a terrible warning to European nations of how a noble vision can be corrupted by the attractions of political power and empire building.

The unanimity of sovereign nations for specific goals is soon replaced by majority decisions by political institutions seeking to centralise power. Independent of and superior to the free nations which so foolishly spawned it, the voracious federal child consumes its parents.

18.

THE NAZI ORIGINS OF
THE EUROPEAN UNION

There is scarcely a single pillar of the present "European" Union which does not have its origins in the blueprint for Europe outlined by Hitler's Nazi regime - with which the French and Italian war time governments were pleased to co-operate.

By far the most ambitious project of today's Eurofederalists is the establishment of a single currency. Although this is paraded as a European currency it is quite clear that, should it ever become a reality, it will in effect be a German currency controlled by a central bank based in Frankfurt - ironically in the former headquarters building of I. G. Farben, the manufacturer of the Nazis' death gas Zyklon B. (One of the industrial contributors to the Nazi paper on the EEC discussed below was Dr Reithinger of I.G. Farben.)

It should be no surprise to the observer of today's "European Community" that its attempts at supranational government differ very little from the last time such an enterprise was undertaken. Then as now the main barrier to a European superstate was the national identities and loyalties of the peoples of Europe. Just as the rise of the nation state produced unparalleled prosperity from inter-nation free trade and new forms of accountability to national parliaments, so it was the individual nations which rose up in both 20th century European wars to frustrate the ambitions of Germany and Italy - the two countries with the shortest and most unstable sense of nationhood.

It is the sense of nationhood which alone produces strong social bonds and a willingness to make sacrifices for the common good. All European attempts to ignore these common identities and bonds have failed comprehensively and catastrophically. Hitler's attempt was perhaps the most horrific since all the power of modern warfare and the civil means of propaganda and suppression were used to bring about the procrustean political and economic union of European nations.

Hitler's plans were collectivist, statist, meticulous and all embracing. We are grateful to Christopher Story, the expert on security and foreign affairs, for printing his translation of the 1942 report of the Nazi "Europäische Wirtschaftsgemeinschaft" (European Economic Community) prepared by the Reich's Economics Minister and President of the Central Bank, Herr Funk and various industrialists, academics and civil servants.(1)

The Reichsmark was to be the leading currency in a German economic area and, after the Dollar the world's second pivotal currency. In July 1940 plans had been drawn up for a "Europabank" through which all European countries controlled by the Nazis would settle payments and which would be the centre of the "closed economic settlement" in Europe.

The Nazis not only planned a common agricultural policy (directed from Berlin rather than from Brussels but with the same principles as today) but also a common monetary policy, a common transport policy ("trans European networks") a common trade policy (ie a Single Market) and - more overt and honestly expressed than today - the direction of labour and state economic control.

Today capital is increasingly directed by the state (in Brussels and national capitals) through government ownership, subsidy and tax incentives. Where capital is forced to go labour is forced to follow. The British worker (as yet only manual labour rather than white collar) is increasingly joining the Italians, Yugoslavs and Turks as the travelling "guest workers" of Europe. In other words we do have the modern equivalent of the Nazi "direction of labour". State control, despite privatisation, has never been more overt, be it through GATT obstruction, the direct and indirect imposition of the "Social Chapter" or massive state subsidies of basic (and even advanced) industries, condoned by a Council of Ministers which frequently overrides market solutions.

Like the modern Europe, the Nazis planned industrial and agricultural capacity (Britain was to have an exclusively agricultural output under a Gauleiter), organised central direction of the European economy (since Maastricht the British Chancellor of the Exchequer has to clear his economic policies with "Europe") the creation of a larger trading area outside the central core (at Heathrow airport there is an entrance marked "European Economic Area"), the establishment of regional committees to report to Berlin, increased European food production regardless of cost in the name of "self sufficiency", common social conditions for all employees, a European motorway network and harmonisation of European Exchange Rates.

In summary a Professor Hunke, President of the Berlin Chamber of Commerce, concluded that the important economic principal was the destruction of the "English system" of free trade based on the nation states. Those of us who have lived and worked in Germany know that even the post war German mind is uncomfortable with free, responsible and atomistic change. They prefer the certainty of the domination of one element by another, properly documented, organised and policed. Freedom of capital, for such a mindset, must mean domination over labour. Neither the German right nor left are convinced of the democratic force of competition and spontaneous methods of social distribution. Therefore the Nazis - and their descendants in the European civil service and continental Governments - choose the domination of labour (and the State which organises labour) over capital. The inevitable next step is to control external trade so that the internal plan cannot be disturbed. This is of course the very process which enslaved Soviet, Eastern Block and Third Reich workers and which destroyed wealth and jobs both in and outside British nationalised industries.

The Nazi Professor Funk expressed this belief in these words which effectively summarise the collectivist notions and economic structures of todays "European" Community.

"...the individual will be replaced by *the people*, the world market will be replaced by *living space* (Lebensraum) and capital will be replaced by the *organisation of labour.*"

The equivalents of these concepts in today's European Union are "solidarity", "the Single Market" and the "Social Chapter". The Nazis, like the European Union, despised Adam Smith and his concepts of free trade, the international division of labour and the "wealth of nations". They prefered organised trade outside the state and organised labour and controlled capital within (as Hunke put it) "an enclosed settlement in Europe".

The important concept of "Lebensraum" which was seen initially as a Nazi idea of space for Germans, was extended to mean Lebensraum for the people of Nazi Europe and it was to embrace a "supplementary colonial economic area" - a concept which lives on today in the European Union's idea of a "European Space". For the Nazis this meant "access" to essential goods and raw materials just as the Energy Committee of the European Parliament and a former Director General of the European Commission have described Britain's (i.e. including Scotland's) North Sea Oil as "European".

The 1930's Europe, like the 1990s version, spoke of "human resources" or "biological resources" just as we might talk of commodities - things to be enhanced and exchanged. The Nazi EEC report has a heading "Exchange of workers on the basis of agreements between Member States". The enhancement of workers includes, under both regimes, state organised and promoted culture. The idea of a Ministry of Culture, common on the continent and promoted in the European Community, is rightly seen as an Orwellian horror by most Britons - but not

121

to those enhancing the commodity of labour through whose increasing Europeanisation more profitable "exchange" will be possible. (see the consequences in the Conclusion below)

One of the most pernicious "European" policies, swallowed hook, line and sinker by the abysmal British Parliament of 1992-3, is the establishment of "Committees of the Regions" - the direct descendant of the Nazis' "European Regional Policy" - which is designed to give regional political and economic organisations direct access to funds raised at the centre (Berlin then, Brussels today) bypassing and therefore rendering irrelevant the National Governments and their own "regional policies". Either national governments raise even more funds to compete with their own taxpayers money channelled through the European central power or they save money by allowing the latter full rein to take over economic and political power in what were once nation states.

This is particularly dangerous in the United Kingdom where the regions of Scotland and Wales are easily tempted to imagine that by "going direct to Europe" they are re-asserting their own national identity against Westminster. It has also been made clear by Brussels that in the new Europe Ireland is one "region" - thus attacking the principal of self determination for the people of Ulster.

But surely Europe is not really threatening the United Kingdom? Surely those Germans who today press for a United Europe cannot be compared to Hitler? Even though the motivations may be different, the effect is already the same - ie the destruction of national constitutions. While railroading Europe into ever greater integration along German lines, Helmut Kohl initially refused to confirm the post war Polish border with Germany and has pursued a hate filled campaign on behalf of the Nazis war time allies Croatia, despite their hideous crimes against the Bosnians. Kohl sees Maastricht as:

> "...a new and decisive stage towards the creation of the United States of Europe."

Kohl has said he would not be satisfied with just a common market for independent sovereign states - how reminiscent of Professor Hunke's Nazi version:

> "There is no sense in putting together all European countries by means of a Customs Union in order to reconstruct for practical purposes a reduced form of the English world economy."

This is of course precisely the line taken today by France and Germany and the European Community. Just as Kohl and Mitterand combined to subsidise and protect state industries in coal, steel, aircraft, airlines and electronics to "build up" Europe to compete so did Hunke take the line:

> "The German Empire has in recent years redirected its economic focus back towards the state sector by means of a considerable degree of self sufficiency because this was the political pre-requisite for the economic independence of Europe."

Where the Nazis drew their inspiration from ancient teutonic myths, the bucolic romanticism of German poets and the collective inevitability of "fate" to construct their hideous empire, today we see Helmut Kohl surrendering to the mythology of "fate".

> "There is no alternative to a policy which aims at combination unless we wish to challenge fate."

Few words are more resonant of the historical German collapse into anti-rationalism, anti-individualism and the herd instinct which has twice destroyed Europe than "das deutsche Schicksal" (German fate or destiny).

To say that the European Community was based on the Nazi version of Europe or that there are parallels would be an understatement. The entire "European" enterprise since the founding of the European Coal and Steel Community in 1951 (and given an enormous boost by the Maastricht Treaty on European Union) is an *exact* replica of the Nazis' ideas for Europe. If there is a major difference it is that unlike Monsieur

Delors, Hitler was at least elected by universal franchise, and by 1942 Hitler spoke for far more (albeit conquered) countries than does the EU today.

But the most significant common thread running through both the Nazi and modern versions of the European State is the contempt for "the English system" - ie a belief in democratic government based on the individual, the nation state and free international trade. The defeat of Hitler and Mussolini was far more significant for its social and economic implications than for its military triumph. The ideas of collectivism, statism, trade protectionism and corporatism are not so physically apparent as the blitz and marching armies, which is why they have so successfully re-established themselves in Europe, under the guise of the "European" Union.

HITLER'S EUROPE	TODAY'S EUROPE
"Europäische Wirtschaft = gemeinschaft" (European Economic Community)	European Economic Community
Lebensraum (living space)	European Space
Collective "access" to basic commodIties.	Common energy, fishing and agricultural policies
European Currency System	European Exchange Rate Mechanism
Europabank (Berlin)	European Central Bank (Frankfurt)
European Regional Principle	Committee of the Regions
Common Labour Policy	Social Chapter
Economic and Trading Agreements	Single Market

HITLER'S EUROPE	TODAY'S EUROPE
European Industrial Economy	Common Industrial Policy
"The transformation of the laws of supply and demand."	Resistance to GATT
"Replacing capital with organised labour"	European Works Councils

(1) International Currency Review, Occasional Paper 4, World Reports
Limited, 108 Horseferry Road, Westminster, London SW1

19.

THE NEW EURO-FASCISTS IN BRUSSELS AND LONDON

Few in the United Kingdom will forget the words of a "European" civil servant called Jacques Delors when, frustrated in his usual quest to dictate to elected representatives what their policies should be, he declared "I will precipitate a crisis". He spoke with the true voice of the fascist state, now experiencing the kind of European revival which must make Hitler and Mussolini laugh in their graves.

Too many hear the term "fascist" either from the mouth of a young socialist as he lambasts those with whom he disagrees or in the specific historical context of the second world war. It is assumed by most that a fascist is either a loud mouthed German with a small moustache and funny salute or a bull necked Italian with more arrogance than power. But fascism is far more subtle and insidious than that and it did not start in 1939 or finish in 1945.

Fascism is the theory that an ordered efficient and happy society can be arranged by scientific planning at the centre by a central party and strong state, dispensing power and privileges to corporate bodies. Those bodies can be corporations, associations of many corporations, trade unions or a congress of trade unions, professional associations or any other collective body which believes that collective will is important, not individual freedom and responsibility. In both left and right wing versions of fascism the producer dominates the consumer, whether the product is political or economic.

Such a society encourages the establishment of committees, parties, collectives, state industrial and investment organisations and a system of imposed authority from the top down. Such systems are typical of state socialism or communism and also of national socialism or fascism. Both types of statist authoritarianism are the enemy of true democrats, liberals, libertarians and (non statist) Conservatives, all of whom promote the freedom and concomitant responsibility of the individual, the family, the community, the nation, the rule of law (as opposed to the rule of the party) and the market economy (as opposed to the diktat of the economic State and its corporate acolytes).

Statist societies tend to appeal to the socially weak and economically insecure who see in collective protectionism the rewards which they could never justify in free competition with their fellow citzens. The planner and corporate organiser also welcome fascist societies since they believe that the whole of society, (in all its complexity and constant change) can be planned, ordered, cajoled and run by wise men (they mean themselves) with wide ranging powers.

Fascist societies cannot tolerate freedom at home and so must outlaw the freedom to trade responsibly abroad. It is just such protectionism and "mercantilism" which have traditionally characterised France and to a smaller extent Germany who have always put the interests of the home market above the liberal internationalist notions of the Anglo Saxon tradition. Indeed it was just such a common approach which allowed those two countries to construct, after the fall of France, the National Socialist "Co-prosperity Zone" based on the ordered division of industrial and agricultural production between France and Germany.

Nazi theorists recognised that they were imposing a system completely different from "the English system" as they called it and it is to just such an anti-British system of state imposition, regulation and "ordered" trade which emanates from the European Commission dominated as it is by German and French civil servants. It is just such an approach which, during the recent GATT negotiations, nearly brought the world to the edge of a disastrous trade war.

One of the distinctive characteristics of this system is that laws are imposed from the top at the behest of business and trade union collectives, designed to enhance their political power and economic wealth, at the cost of the freedom and self sufficiency of the individual, who has nothing more than his (totally emasculated) vote at infrequent elections.

There have been many recent examples of statist and fascist behaviour in the United Kingdom in recent years. One of the most insidious of fascist practices is the imposition of retrospective law, that is laws which allow the dispossession or prosecution of those for doing what, at the time of their action, was perfectly legal. By passing the infamous "leasehold reform" legislation the Conservative Government in 1993 was guilty of such a practice. Indeed by requiring that property owners (freeholders) sell to their leaseholders on demand the "Conservative" government has come close to marxist principles. The right to private property, the right to the protection of contract and the right to be protected from retrospective legislation were all infringed by this act of a so called "democratic" party.

During the same parliamentary session the speaker of the House of Commons took it upon herself to threaten the law courts who were considering the legality of the Maastricht Treaty (the Rees Mogg case). Our judges have a vital constitutional role in a free society. It is not they who threaten democracy but the Parliament which gives away the powers of the people without consulting them and a government which signs away 800 years of Parliamentary statute under "royal prerogative".

When, at the Conservative Party conference in 1992 a group of Young Conservatives organised an anti Maastricht meeting, a group of pro Maastricht members of the "Tory Reform Group" appeared at the back of the hall to hurl abuse. At the end of the meeting this group of some 10 men stood still in their serried ranks, partly obstructing the only exit from the room. In similar vein physical violence and abuse were used within the House of Commons against anti Maastricht MPs as they tried to vote. (see in particular the book by Teresa Gorman MP "Bastards") These are indeed excellent physical demonstrations of the statist, collectivist, anti individual logic which permeates the entire Euro-federalist crusade. They coerce individuals with physical acts just as the embryo Eurostate coerces the nation states of Europe and just as the British government coerced the British people when refusing a vote on Maastricht. Such violent petulance is the physical mirror image of the abusive words hurled by Eurofanatics like Jaques Delors, Edward Heath and Hugh Dykes MP. It was a Foreign Office Minister responsible for negotiating the Maastricht Treaty, Tristan Garel Jones MP, who attacked in a most vicious manner a fellow Conservative MP, saying he wanted to "see your body floating down the river as an example to enemies of the State".

Typical of statist and fascist policies within the European Community are the shutting of the most advanced steel works in Europe (operated by responsible free trading British steel companies) and a £28m fine on British Steel while billions of pounds are granted in subsidies to State owned steel in France, Italy and Germany (the three centres of economic fascism in the last war). As British Coal shuts mines producing at £45 per ton, Germany employs 5 times as many miners producing at £112 per ton, and refuses to import British coal.

The entire French economy is a massive interconnecting labyrinth of state ownership, state subsidy or funding by state owned or dominated banks. This is the kind of logic which has destroyed hundreds of thousands of British jobs in airlines, computers, coal and steel and it is the logic prevalent around the table of the Council of Ministers which daily prevents the Commission imposing free trading policies on the industries of the EC.

It is also evident that Britain, by being increasingly locked into the grotesque trading and fiscal systems of Europe now loses out threefold. First jobs and profits are lost as other operators in the EC market get unfair subsidies, secondly it is our money (as the EC's second biggest financier) which is being used to subsidise European companies and destroy our industries and thirdly our markets in third countries suffer from competition from state manipulated European companies and welfare and taxation burdens imposed on British companies from Brussels.

Every day that passes the constitutional outrage of the Maastricht Treaty is becoming clearer. Recently the British Government was ordered (by an alien power, over which the British voter has no control) to give part time workers the same privileges as full time workers, that companies must consult workers on matters of business ownership, that, despite previous agreements, maximum working hours are to be imposed by the EC and companies must pay higher maternity benefits (at the cost of the single, childless and old).

The governing party in the United Kingdom mentioned no such policies in its manifesto, the Government actually opposes these policies and Parliament has passed no such legislation. And yet the British people have had these laws imposed upon them.

Whether these laws are reasonable or desirable is irrelevant to the fact that they are palpably not OUR laws. In the not too distant future laws emanating from a Europe dominated by communists or fascists (National Front in France, Fascist Party in Italy or Republicans in Germany) could be imposed upon the British people, using the same "European" legislation.

When the "European" Community is not imposing laws on the British people, it is preventing the passage of laws deemed necessary by the British Government. When a number of American tourists were killed in a coach on its way to Canterbury, the Government admitted that had seat belts been installed (as was the Government's policy) few would have died. But the European Community had repeatedly refused to accept such laws - while simultaneously insisting that all coaches, with or without seat belts, could not be prevented from entering any member state. In other words the British Government was powerless to act since to impose legislation only on British coach owners would have allowed non British coaches (without seat belts) to undercut and therefore destroy their markets.

British politicians seem to have no idea of why we went to war against Hitler and his regime. It was not because he was a Nazi, nor because he persecuted his own people nor even because he practised genocide (not widely known in 1939) but because he tried to impose his rule on the nation states of Europe. Despite his military aggression and the slaughter of millions Hitler never succeeded in making or suspending our laws as the "European" Court now does almost daily, nor did he ever control who could enter, reside in and vote in our country. Even his bombs did not decimate our steel, coal and car industries as the European Community has done.

These latest cases of legal impositions on our country expose the fraudulent nature of the British "opt out" from the social chapter of the Maastricht Treaty. They also contradict absolutely the "subsidiarity" principle of the Maastricht Treaty which, according to John Major, was to give us more control over our own legislation. Needless to say those who actually READ the Treaty (unlike the Foreign and Home Secretaries at the time) knew that this was not the case.

The Maastricht Treaty in fact accelerated the daily destruction of our democratic rights and the national sovereignty for which so much British (and Commonwealth) blood was so recently spilled.

This Government and the Parliament which has destroyed our nation and our democracy will live in infamy. The British people will not rest until they have regained their country, their Parliamentary sovereignty and their right to self government.

20.

THE THREAT FROM GERMANY TODAY

The American journalist Dorothy Thompson spent much time in Germany in 1940 talking to Nazi theorists about their plans for Europe. In the *Herald Tribune* of 31st May 1940 she wrote:

> "The Germans count upon political power following economic power. Territorial changes do not concern them because there will be no "France" or "England" except as language groups. Little immediate concern is felt regarding political organisations...No nation will have control of its own financial or economic system or its customs."

One could not imagine a better description of the present German plans for the European Union (as envisaged in the Maastricht Treaty, signed by the British government).

At the end of the 1940s and early 1950s there were various well funded Nazi organisations in Europe in particular Madrid and Stuttgart. The American writer T.H. Tetens made a detailed study of their output. He wrote:

> "The nazi theory after World War II was that if the Germans lost their sovereignty it would be a smart idea to talk the other nations into a scheme in which they would also have to give up their sovereignty....Germany had lost territory and prestige but it would profit in a European Union."

In senior American political circles in the early 50s there were many who saw what the Clinton administration has today failed to understand. Senator Hickenlooper at the Foreign Affairs Committee hearings March 1952:

> "the French the British and the Italians thought that if they took Germany into a comparatively integrated Europe... German industry would completely dominate the economy of Europe and the rest of them would be more or less economic satellites of Germany within about 10 years. Within 10 years the Germans would have obtained by peace what they could not obtain by two wars."

Naturally the subsequent market economic emphasis of the EEC combined with the division of Germany between communist east and capitalist west prevented political integration and the German domination which Western Europe had feared. But since the 1986 Single European Act, the 1992 Maastricht Treaty and the reunification of Germany under the aggressively European integrationist Chancellor Kohl the political domination by 80 million Germans of EU institutions has begun. Intent on large scale economic, social and political intervention German political leadership has already caused dangerous tensions both within Germany and throughout Europe.

The whole basis of a statist, interventionist and protectionist Europe which has been the aim of Germans - and many Frenchmen - since the end of the 19th century has now been reconstructed under the guise of "Europe". Needless to say the "European" community today represents only one third of the nations of Europe but through sleight of hand, lies, deceit and implied economic protectionism against those who remain outside, Brussels, Bonn and Paris believe they can cajole many other nations into the "Union". Once the honey pot of subsidies and apparent "free trade" have attracted the naive nations of western Europe and the impoverished nations of eastern Europe into the European Union then the statist and protectionist core will tighten their political control and withdrawal will be impossible. In addition, having reduced the number of sovereign free trading European nations the EU "core" eliminates the logic of an association of nations

OUTSIDE the union. There therefore remains no check or challenge to its power block concept.

Before the first world war Germany planned a Europe-wide coal and steel combine. After the first war they tried to establish a European Steel cartel; in 1940 after the defeat of France Hitler and the collaborationist Vichy regime (in which François Mitterand played a significant role) established a joint industrial system; After the second world war this formed the basis of the 1951 European Coal and Steel Community which in turn formed the core of the European Economic Community created in 1956 by the Treaty of Rome. The EEC therefore represented not a clean break with the past and a step towards a liberal internationalist future but rather it was a logical and political continuation of the "continental system" which had been the German aim in the first half of the 20th century.

German defeat in two world wars - with the considerable help of a liberal free trading, democratic America - allowed free nations to flourish in Europe. It was the Atlanticist NATO which protected the fragile democracies and infant parliaments of post war western Europe. It was British and American notions of democratic accountability, constitutional rights, the non political rule of law and international free trade which became the basis of European prosperity and political stability.

This peace was itself brought about only by free nations acting together to defeat the supranational, imperialist, protectionist power block which the Nazis in Germany, the Fascists in Italy and collaborators in France sought to establish. But today we see the re-emergence in European institutions of all the characteristics of fascist Europe. There is growing anti-American and anti-British feeling in both France and Germany. Trade and social agreements are made under an ostensible rule of law and then broken with impunity. Lip service is paid to the democracy of market forces but then the political state imposes its will at the cost of competitive industry and free consumers.

134

Italy blatantly ignores all rules on milk production, is fined about £1,300m and refuses to pay, threatening to block the entire EC budget. The rule of law is compromised and they are let off £500m of the fine originally imposed.

France, Germany, Italy and Spain continue massive state subsidies of coal, steel, computers and airlines, destroying British companies and jobs in these sectors on a scale of which even Hitler would have been proud. The European Commission, charged with enforcing fair trade and the rule of law is, like the United Kingdom itself, simply outvoted in the Council of Ministers. In other words the whole point of the Single European Act as sold to Mrs Thatcher by Geoffrey Howe et al (ie that majority voting would INCREASE market forces and fair trade) has been turned on its head. Such voting now overrides the free traders and liberals, compounding the sclerosis of state subsidy, dumping and protectionism.

A British company which imports silk from China has been threatened with the prohibition of further imports by the EC Commission. These regulations apply in other EC countries but they are typically circumvented or ignored. Writing to the prime Minister the managing director of the company, whose very existence is threatened said:

> "The Germans, when presented with the new rules concerning silk stated that they "did not understand the text" and ignored it...The Spanish are importing silk through the Canary Islands....The French interpret these rules selectively"

It has been suggested that the British should learn to "bend" the rules of the EC just as other countries and companies do. There is apparently some notion about "proportionality" in the application of laws - that if the application of a law produces a cost out of all proportion to the original intention of the law then it should be ignored! Needless to say this is a recipe for chaos and illegality. Such an approach would lead rapidly from the marginal case to the entire system of law.

Only in a fundamentally fascist organisation (in which corporate, institutional and state interests override the rule of law) could an official of the European Court say to an American journalist:

> "Britain has an almost depersonalised concept of the law in that they blindly obey the law even when it does not suit them politically. Almost nobody else in the world does that and certainly no other member states do."

This short paragraph could be the subject of several volumes of legal, philosophical and political analysis but the thousands of words would merely add up to an incredulous gasp of outrage that anyone could say such things in a democratic country, in Europe, in the last years of the twentieth century.

And yet those who have lived for any length of time in other European countries, never mind elsewhere, know all too well that concepts like the separation of powers, the rule of law, fairness (there is no such word in German, French or Italian) or even popular sovereignty are hardly well established principles. Individual voters are treated with contempt in Germany where party apparatchiks rule and individual MPs dare not speak even their own objections never mind those of their constituents. Indeed many German MPs have no constituents since half are elected by a list system through proportional representation. As in the so-called European parliament if an MP dies there isn't even a bye-election! In France parliament is the plaything of the presidency.

But let us return to the official of the highest court in the European Community - a court which, by its own admission, is less an arbitrator and more a creator of new law (and an overrider of national laws!). And yet this official cannot grasp the very basis of law - that it is non political and that political bodies, like governments, are beneath it; or that it is precisely because the law is "depersonalised" that it is respected and not open to manipulation on a case by case basis. Or that to obey the law, far from being "blind" is an open, rational acceptance of social constraint for free people.

Greece (which held the presidency of the European Union for the first half of 1994) has for some time been technically at war with another European state - Macedonia. It has been blockading that state which, according to international law, is an act of war. Nevertheless, during the Greek Presidency of the European Union, the "European Court of Justice" simply refused to act against Greece. Both the European Commission and the British government are appalled at the court ruling but they can do nothing about it - just as the British government can do nothing about its multi-million pound annual subsidy to the Greek economy!

We learn that two Greek officials jailed for their part in a maize fraud have been pardoned and released from jail by the Greek parliament. One has become an MP the other is head of the state owned Bank of Attica.

All these scandals show how a Franco-German dominated Europe which in peace and war has pursued a fascist social and economic system, now achieves through political, rather than military power, the debasement of the rule of law. This should come as no surprise given the post war role of those who learned their political trade under the Nazis. The institutions and philosophy of the EU during the catastrophic 1980s were dominated by the ideas of Jacques Delors. His youth politics were spent in the "Compagnons de France", a movement which was the first to be officially created and financed by the collaborationist Vichy regime. "To govern is to plan" is a favourite phrase of Delors, an embodiment of the collectivist and capitalist which epitomises socio-economic fascism.

Equally dominant in the EU of the 1980s was Francois Mitterand, 14 years in office as president of France, a collaborator in the Vichy regime and the recipient of its highest award. The Italian politicians who bounced Mrs Thatcher into more federalist integration (aided by Geoffrey Howe) have been arrested or investigated for fraud and corruption. It was a senior Italian official responsible for the

Common Agricultural Policy in Italy who jumped to his death from the European Commission headquarters building in Brussels. In Britain the pro-integrationist, pro-ERM Confederation of British Industry now rejects as catastrophic everything which it previously recommended - although it has now expressed its preference for the abolition of the Pound.

The CBI is of course the prime mover in the rise of corporatism and statism in the United Kingdom. And it was to that audience that The European Social Affairs Commissioner Padraig Flynn addressed the subject of the Social Chapter. His speech was reported as follows in the *Evening Standard* of 8th November 1994:

> "...business leaders were urged to side step the opt out Britain negotiated from the European Social Chapter at Maastricht by striking collective agreements with trade unions on controversial areas of employment policy. Padraig Flynn, Europe's Social Affairs Commissioner, told the conference that this could take the initiative away from politicians and place it in the hands of management and labour."

A better example of fascism in action is impossible to imagine.

As the UK Foreign Office and CBI sink further into the Euro-fascist abyss the realisation of what has been planned for so long and is now well under way is beginning to dawn on the British people. The popular tide is turning violently against a federal Europe, against the arrogance of corporatism and against the state dominated economic and financial manipulation which is the lot of a people deprived of their democratic institutions. The return to the evils of the 1930s is now no longer a danger but a reality. Fascism has not yet caused the economic collapse and political upheavals which lead inevitably to militarism, social persecution and war but such convulsions are now not far off.

Even a cursory analysis of the governing party in Germany today - the Christian Democratic Union under Helmut Kohl - shows the extent to which German nationalism, not German internationalism, is the driving force behind their aggressive policy of "European Integration".

The recently published policy paper proposed rapid development of a federal Europe of a core group of countries. Against all democratic principles those countries like Denmark, Italy and Britain which do not wish to proceed along such lines would effectively be excluded. In other words either Europe acts as Germany wishes or "Europe" will mean something else and those not willing to obey will be thrown out of "Europe".

Barely disguised in Germany's rush to European integration is the ever present notion that Europe is threatened by "nationalism" - but not of course by the aggression of German nationalism. Let us consider these three contrasting quotes from the recent CDU/CSU report "Reflections on European Policy" authored by Wolfgang Schäuble, a German nationalist and fanatical Euro-integrationist (imagine this combination in the UK ?). First the contempt for other nations:

> "the notion of the unsurrenderable sovereignty of the *État Nation* still carries weight although this sovereignty has long since become an empty shell."

Then the approval of German nationalism (despite the fact that it was only German nationalism which has proved a threat to Europe!)

> "...our citizens know full well that Germany's interests can only be realised in, with, through Europe and that far from imposing a threat to the nation this in fact safeguards its essence because it safeguards its future."

then the threat:

> "If (West) European integration were not to progress, Germany might be called upon or be tempted by its own security constraints to try to effect the stabilisation of Eastern Europe on its own and in the traditional manner."

Apart from the overt political and even military threat in this sentence it is interesting to note the use of the word "stabilisation". Central to the vocabulary of German politics, or corporatism in general and of the European Union in particular are concepts like "control", or "stable". The CBI uses the word "stable" when it talks about exchange rates - despite having unleashed the most destabilising economic period of recent times when they embraced the idea of "stable" exchange rates in the European exchange rate mechanism (ERM).

When fascists talk about "control" they mean control by themselves - and of those elements which will affect them. It matters not how such controls drive others to the wall by causing massive upheavals elsewhere.

Consider the arrogance of Theo Waigel the German Finance Minister who said about the location of the European Central Bank:

> "Either the ECB comes to Frankfurt or else the organisation will not get off the ground."

Nor could we assume that the German Social Democratic Party is any different. Had they won the recent German elections their even more integrationist, statist and Europe-wide policies might have been less overt than the blustering bullying of Helmut Kohl but it would have been no less potent and destructive of the interests of the United Kingdom.

The former SDP leader Helmut Schmidt, whose close relationship with President Giscard d'Estaing promoted further European integration, has now founded a nationalist organisation to define and present German national interest. It is called the German National Foundation. This may have the best intentions - ie to deflect dangerous nationalism into more sobre nationalist and democratic avenues but the fact that such a strategy is necessary is a direct result of the supra nationalist strategy which both left and right wing parties have pursued in

Germany in their drive to European integration and the suppression of independent national interests.

The more Bonn and Brussels have suppressed legitimate national feeling (I prefer the word nationist to national) by the promotion of political and constitutional integration in Europe the more even moderate German nationalism, never mind the more virulent kind, has been antagonised. The more Bonn and Brussels have attempted economic and financial integration (as opposed to competitive free trading markets) the more sclerotic and destabilised the European market has become and the higher unemployment has risen, providing yet another fertile ground for the worst elements of German nationalism.

In this respect the German government has much in common with the British which recommends each further step towards integration - and therefore loss of sovereign British control - on the basis that it will help to solve the crisis which the last integrationist step caused. If their Euro-integrationist policies succeed they pursue them more fanatically. If they fail they then call on more integration since "Britain cannot tackle such a crisis if it is isolated". In other words the policy is based on an argument they cannot lose. An argument which you cannot lose is no argument at all.

German leaders have in the name of "Europe" ruthlessly pursued their own national interest while pretending all the time that only an integrated Europe can quell their own "dangerous nationalist elements" (see von Richthofen above in the Introduction). This hypocrisy arises out of German schizophrenia - so graphically demonstrated on the Queen's visit to Germany where the Union Jack was waved but instead of the German flag - of which so many were apparently ashamed - Germans waved the "European" flag. A country so ashamed of its own identity is hardly a comfortable partner in an association of nations.

It is not the nation state or even nationalism which has proved a threat to European peace and prosperity, it is German nationalism combined with attempts to forge a German

141

dominated supranational Eurostate. Those nations which cannot live in peace with themselves cannot be trusted to be modest and cooperative participants in a European Union, especially one which, by their collectivist and protectionist policies, they will necessarily dominate.

The two world wars this century were not principally wars between nations for territory but between two entirely different world views. The continental system represents protectionism, statism and dirigisme. Trade for them is not an emancipated process of fair exchange between free nations but, in the words of a German statesman "the continuation of war by other means". That system was and is opposed by the anglo saxon principles of free trade, the importance of the individual (and hence democracy) within national societies and the primacy of the nation in international affairs.

The far more fundamental "war" between these two philosophies is being waged today. The weapons are not bullets, tanks aircraft and bombs but treaties, directives, taxes and regulations. The enemy does not destroy our country he removes the very definition of our country. The enemy does not sack our parliament, he merely takes all democratic power from it, leaving an empty shell as an entertainment for tourists. The enemy does not remove our sovereign Queen he keeps her in place as the titular head of a vassal state. The enemy does not abolish the rule of law but he emasculates our courts and imposes his own laws. The threat to our country is no less today than in the 1930s - indeed it is greater and more insidious because the threat is so well hidden.

If this great nation does not wake up today, it will not exist tomorrow.

21.

CHRONOLOGY OF THE PASSAGE OF THE MAASTRICHT BILL

1992 May 7

First reading in the Commons.

1992 May 20-21

Second reading in the Commons. Liberal Democrats voted with Government; Labour Party officially abstained.

1992 June 2

Danes rejected the Treaty in a referendum.

1992 Nov 4

Government won the paving debate to allow committee stage of bill by 319 votes to 316. Liberal Democrats voted with the Government.

1993 Feb 22

Attorney-General announced that even if the House carried Labour amendment to reinstate the Social Chapter, the Treaty would still be ratified.

1993 Mar 22

Call for Referendum rejected at the end of 163 hours of debate in Committee.

1993 May 4

Facing certain defeat from combined Labour, Liberal Democrat and Conservative Euro-sceptics, Mr. Hurd announced he would accept an Amendment to delete the United Kingdom's social chapter opt-out since it would have 'no legal effect' on the Government's ability to ratify.

1993 May 20

Government secured Third Reading in Commons by a majority of 180 votes (292-112) with 66 Labour and 41 Conservative MP's voting against the Government.

1993 July 12-14

Lords' Report Stage. On last of three days Lord Blake's amendment, calling for a referendum, defeated by 445 votes to 176.

1993 July 20

Lords' third reading secured for the Bill by 141 votes to 29. Royal Assent obtained that evening.

1993 July 22

A Labour amendment to a Government motion noting the policy of HMG on the non-adoption of the protocol on social policy was defeated by the Speaker's casting vote, after a tie of 317-317 (it was later discovered that Labour's amendment had in fact been lost 316-317). The Government's own motion was lost 324-316, with 23 Conservative MP's voting against the Government and one abstaining. Prime Minister announced the tabling of a revised motion next day, making it also a vote of confidence in the Government, thus threatening a General Election.

1993 July 23

Government defeated Labour's identically worded anti opt-out amendment by 339 votes to 301. Carried its own vote of confidence with 339 votes to 299.

1993 July 30

Lord Rees-Mogg's High Court judicial review of the legality of the ratification of the Treaty failed.

1993 Aug 2

The United Kingdom delivered the instrument of ratification in Rome, purporting this to be 'in accordance with its constitutional requirements'.

1993 Oct 12

The German Constitutional Court in Karlsruhe interprets the Treaty both in respect of EC funding and an EMU opt-out in a way unprovided for in the text. The President of the Federal Republic of Germany nonetheless claims ratification. Documents are forwarded to Rome.

1993 Nov 1

The *soi-disant* European Union purports to be now in being.

1994 March 7th

Rodney Atkinson and Norris McWhirter issue press release which demonstrates that the Maastricht Treaty ostensibly approved by the German Constitutional Court is not the Treaty signed at Maastricht and that therefore the entire ratification process was invalid.

22.

ROLL OF HONOUR

Peers voting for a referendum on Maastricht in the division that took place in the House of Lords on Wednesday 14th July 1993.

Dukes (3)

Devonshire
Roxburghe
Somerset

Marquesses (5)

Aberdeen and Temair
Ailesbury
Huntly
Salisbury
Zetland

Earls (34)

Alexander of Tunis
Baldwin of Bewdley
Bathhurst
Bradford
Buchan
Clanwilliam
Crawford and Balcarries
Effingham
Errol
Essex
Gainsborough
Granard
Haddington

Kintore
Liverpool
Lloyd-George of Dwyfor
Lovelace
Macclesfield
Munster
Nelson
Northesk
Onslow
Peel
Portland
Radnor
Ranfurley
Romney
St Germans
Shrewsbury
Sondes
Spencer
Suffolk and Berkshire
Woolton
Yarlborough

Viscounts (14)

Buckmaster
Chilston
Combermere
Cowdray

Craigavon
Cross
Hampden
Hardinge
Ingleby
Knutsford
Massereene and Ferrard
Mountgarret
Scarsdale
Tonypandy

Barons (112) (*life Baron)

Acton
Annaly
Asbourne
Bambury of Southam
Bauer*
Belhaven and Stenton
Beloff*
Biddulph
Birdwood
Blake*
Blyth
Brandon of Oakbrook
Braybrooke
Brimelow*
Brooks of Tremorfa*
Bruce of Donington*
Burton
Buxton of Alsa*
Campbell of Eskan
Clwyd
Cochrane of Cults
Cocks of Hartcliffe*
Cornwallis
Craigmyles
Cunliffe
Dacre of Glanton*
De Saumarez
Derwent
Donaldson of Lymington

Dormand of Easington*
Dormer
Elphinstone
Fairfax of Cameron
Fisher
Fitt*
Galpern*
Gisborough
Glenamara
Glenarthur
Glenconner
Goodman*
Gray
Hamilton of Dalzell
Hardinge of Penhurst
Harmar-Nicholls*
Harris of High Cross*
Harvey of Tasburgh
Hirshfield*
Hollick*
HolmPatrick
Howie of Troon*
Jakobovits*
Jay*
Jeffreys
Jenkins of Putney*
Kagan*
Kenilworth
Kilbracken
Kindersley
Leigh
Mancroft
Margadale
Middleton
Milne
Mishcon*
Molloy*
Monson
Moore of Wolvercote*
Moran
Morris
Morris of Kenwood

Napier and Ettrick
Parkinson*
Parry*
Pearson of Rannoch*
Pitt of Hampstead*
Porritt
Rankeillour
Rathcreedan
Rayleigh
Rees-Mogg*
Rennell
Rodney
Saint Oswald
Sandys
Savile
Sharp of Grimsdyke
Skidelsky*
Smith*
Spens
Stafford
Stanley of Alderley
Stoddart of Swindon*
Stokes*
Sudeley
Swansea
Swinfen
Tebbit*
Teviot
Tombs*
Torphichen
Trevethin and Oaksey
Tryon
Vinson*
Wedderburn of Charlton*
Wedgwood
Whaddon*
Willoughby de Broke
Wise
Wolfson of Sunningdale*
Wrenbury

Baronesses (8)

Castle of Blackburn*
Cox*
Jeger*
Mallalieu*
Oppenheim-Barnes*
Strange
Thatcher*
Wharton

CONCLUSION

The historian A.J.P. Taylor wrote of the British Constitution "In our flexible system anything is constitutional which is tolerated by contemporaries." The question now facing the British people and their "democratic representatives" is whether this "flexibility" is a pragmatic strength or a fatal flaw in what (until the Maastricht Treaty) was the British Constitution.

It is evident even to the layman that a house, once built, can tolerate painting and decorating, the expansion of some rooms and the contraction of others - but without a firm structure and sound foundations it will not long remain a house. So it is in the United Kingdom that we can tolerate changing laws without changing the rule of law. We can expand the franchise without destroying voting rights. We can trade with, communicate with and exchange visitors with other nations without sacrificing our own nation. We can agree to international codes of behaviour, laws of contract, shipping rights and much else which facilitate inter-nation trade without making our parliament subservient to an alien authority. But we cannot allow others to take over the rights of our parliament, nor to make or suspend our laws, nor to decide who can enter, reside in and vote in our country. Nor can we permit others in the name of a "single market" to prevent us legislating on matters of safety, or to allocate to themselves fishing rights in our internationally recognised territorial limits. The loss of British fishing grounds during Heath's negotiations for entry into the EEC was a straight forward destruction of property rights - it was nothing to do with free and fair trade.

Just as the British people were being dispossessed of their historical fishing grounds as the EEC ensured us of an increase in profitable trade, so at Maastricht, while talking of regaining our sovereignty through "subsidiarity" the European Community was bent on destroying the British Constitution.

It is no surprise that the United Kingdom should be the centre of resistance to the new Eurostate. For it was only the existence of Britain as an independent nation state which turned back the supranational fascism of the 1930s. Virtually all the other member states were either ruled by fascists or conquered by fascists within the living memory of anyone over 55. They have been led to believe that that European tragedy was caused by "nationalism". It was not, it was caused by international fascism - not dissimilar to international communism in its imperial desires, its glorif ication of the party, the corporation and the state and in its contempt for the individual, his vote and his freedom.

The true tragedy of the "European" Community is that the whole upheaval, the destruction of democratic rights, the constitutional outrages and the imposition of an alienating artificial superstate on the fearful peoples of free nations is all completely unnecessary. Indeed the whole enterprise is a step backwards into the disasters of the Soviet Union and Yugoslavia. Even the federal United States, with the largest financial deficit in the history of the world, is showing signs of moral decadence, long term economic decline and social breakdown, although even the USA over the last two decades has exceeded the performance of the "European" Community in terms of employment, investment and wealth creation.

Just as in Britain the unholy alliance between failing Government and failing corporations responded to economic decline after the war by multiplying "tripartite" organisations for the "organisation" of markets, industry, prices, investment and industrial relations, so a similar process is under way today in the "European" Community. "Europe", as defined by the fifteen members of the Community, has been in long term decline and the reaction of those responsible for that decline is to intervene, organise, legislate and regulate. In today's Europe

150

the new corporatist state (or "state capitalism") desires to control on the one hand every lever of business and yet on the other subject nations and cultures to laissez faire destruction in order to ease the sale of goods and people. It is this combination of materialist freedom and cultural, economic and social control which, for the corporatist, necessitates the destruction of the nation state.

As I write this conclusion there is news of the death on a Belgian motorway of a number of unemployed Britons who naively set out to find work "in Europe" where there was none in Britain. Much of the capital which might have employed those men at home has been seduced by Government and Euro propaganda into areas of the "Single Market" where the capital owners could have much less knowledge than in their home markets. Where capital goes labour must follow. Mobility of labour sounds an enticing prospect to the Euro civil servant or British accountant looking forward to a few (voluntary) years in Rome or London or Brussels. But the reality for the bulk of the labour market is the nomadic life, mass migrations, family break up and cultural alienation. As Rodney Atkinson warned in the pamphlet *Your Country Your Democracy* (1992) British workers are becoming the guest workers of Europe, divorced from their friends, family, communities and nation.

The nation state is the source of cultural identity and social cohesion on the one hand and the very reason for the unprecedented growth in inter-nation trade which has created so much and distributed so widely the "wealth of nations". While the developing countries in South East Asia, the former Soviet Union, India and Latin America learn these lessons to their increasing advantage, "Europe" is hell bent on a return to the dark ages of state domination and collectivist failure.

The politicians who secretly instigated and negotiated this enterprise will never be forgiven by their electorates. We can only pray that the end will come through democratic means and not by yet another violent conflagration in Europe.

In valedictory messages to the British people Raymond Seitz, retiring American ambassador to the Court of St James, gave conflicting advice.

In what was seen by some as an "anti-Eurosceptic" remark he said that the United Kingdom was "part of Europe" and the US administration would tend to see Europe as a whole, with communication being conducted "between one continent and another". (Perhaps Brussels or London should take a similar approach to North America and give equal prominence to Ottawa and Mexico City when discussing the interests of the United States.)

But in rather more heartfelt tones Seitz concluded a speech on his family's return to Omaha beach, where his father had led a regiment on D Day. In a bright silver dollar given to him as a boy by the present Commandant of the Royal Military Academy at Sandhurst, Seitz saw "chapter after chapter of friendship between two great peoples who continue to write their own fine Book of Nations" (note the word nations).

Needless to say these are two entirely conflicting positions. As a "Eurosceptic", I hope that Mr Seitz's heart, expressing the love of our sovereign nation, will overrule his diplomatic head which seems bent on subsuming our nation into the Eurofederalist mire.

But there is a far more dangerous issue at stake. For on Omaha beach Mr Seitz's father helped to put an end, not just to a fascist military power and political tyranny but to the entire social and economic system which underlay them. Today that system is being gradually and skillfully rebuilt under the guise of the federal "European Union" and unless the United States recognises the threat to its own interests from a statist, corporatist (and therefore protectionist) Eurostate we may yet have to return to Omaha beach.

Ambassaador Seitz, when he thinks of two nations and Omaha beach, has sound instincts. European nations are as much a bulwark against European collectivism and fascism today as they were when they combined with the USA to defeat Nazi Germany. For when the Nazis opposed "the English system" of nation based free trade they included in their strictures the liberal instincts and market capitalism of the United States. It will never be in the interests of the United States to subsume into a federalist (German and French dominated) Europe the one stable and consistent voice of liberal nationhood. If Raymond Seitz and the American administration think they can afford to ignore the nation of Adam Smith, Nelson, Wellington and Churchill, then America and Europe will have set out on a dark and dangerous path.

Appendix I
Further notes on the Bilderbergers

The British Foreign and Commonwealth Office, when asked by a journalist what they knew about the Bilderberg group denied its existence, saying, in cleverly chosen weasle words "...we can find no trace of the Bilderberg Group in any of our reference works on international organisations". In fact the British Foreign Office has on many occasions paid for British Bilderbergers to attend Bilderberg conferences.

The *Financial Times* journalist C. Gordon Tether was sacked by that haven of modern statism and corporatism because he refused to have his long running "Lombard" column censored. The *Financial Times* had removed sections of his column refering to the Bilderberg group and the Lockheed scandal (which involved the founder of the Bilderbergers Prince Bernhard of the Netherlands). The Lombard column was the world's longest running daily column and Gordon Tether's subsequent industrial case against the *Financial Times* was also the longest - some 18 months before the might of the *Financial Times* conquered a principled journalist.

The strictly confidential minutes of the first Bilderberg conference in 1954 contained the following words which indicate rather more than an unofficial discussion club: "..to **evolve an international order which would look beyond the present day crisis. When the time is ripe our present concepts of world affairs should be extended to the whole world.**"

As Benjamin Disraeli remarked:

"The world is governed by very different personages from what is imagined by those who are not behind the scenes."

Appendix II
The costs of a Euro-MP

It costs the British taxpayer £919,961 per annum to finance a British member of the European Parliament. The total annual cost of sustaining Britain's 87 MEPs on the Brussels gravy train has now reached a cool £80 million. It costs the British taxpayer more than three times as much to maintain an MEP as a Westminster MP.

	£MEP's	£MP's
Salary of support staff	365,961	47,926
Rent allowance	88,007	15,207
Secretarial costs	77,954	41,321
Travel costs	77,249	15,207
Office equipment	71,605	2,765
Other staff costs	45,679	27,650
Other costs	40,035	nil
Office running costs	36,508	39,300
Basic salary	33,189	33,189
Subscriptions to parliamentary bodies	28,395	4,301
Publications	19,048	13,210
Salaries and pensions (ex basic)	12,698	912
'General' expenses	11,993	19,201
Security	11,640	18,894
Total	**£919,961**	**£297,272**

THE AUTHORS

Norris McWhirter CBE MA is joint founder of the *Guinness Book of Records* (which at 77 million copies sold is second only to the Bible) a Director of Guinness Publishing and Chairman of the Freedom Association. After War service in the Royal Navy he represented Oxford, Scotland and Britain as a sprinter. He worked as a journalist on *The Observer* and as a commentator for BBC radio and television. He has been a co-presenter of the BBC's "Record Breakers" since 1972 and of "Guinness Hall of Fame" since 1986 and he was a member of the Sports Council from 1970 to 1973. Among other charitable work he is a trustee of the Police Convalescent and Rehabilitation Trust. He contested Orpington in 1964 and 1966. Other publications include *Athletics World*, the *Dunlop Book of Facts* and the *Guinness Book of Answers*.

Rodney Atkinson BA MSc MIL studied at the Universities of Durham and Newcastle upon Tyne before becoming a lecturer at the University of Mainz in Germany. He returned to take up posts in merchant banking in the City of London before starting his own businesses in property, commercial conferences and publishing. He is the founder and owner of Public Issue Conferences, an internationally praised political economist and has been an occasional adviser to Government Ministers. He is the author of four books and some sixty articles and policy papers which have sold in 16 countries. He has written for, among others, *The Guardian*, *The Daily Telegraph*, *The Times*, *The Financial Times* and the *Wall Street Journal* (Europe) and has been a frequent commentator on political and economic affairs on television and radio.

INDEX

acquis communautaire, 33, 60, 61, 72, 74, 93, 112

Act of Union (see Union with Scotland Act)

Action Committee for the United States of Europe, 15

Adams, Gerry, 102

Airlines, 135

agriculture, 2

allegiance, 1, 11, 62, 80, 96, 98

America, 1, 65, 67, 107-117, 130, 134, 153

American Civil War, 48

American Committee on a United Europe, 16, 17

American Union, 35, 48

Anglo Saxon, 2, 25, 30, 142

appeasement, 71

Ashdown, Paddy, 2

asylum, 84

Athens, 82

Atkinson, Rodney, 7, 36, 53, 53, 55, 77, 107, 145, 151, 153

Atlanticist, 68, 134

Attlee, Clem, 58

Attorney General, 47, 79, 80

Austria-Hungary, 104

Axon, Miss P., 52

Baker, Kenneth, 52

Bank of Attica, 137

Bank of England, 4, 75, 77

Barber judgement, 32

BBC, 71, 91

Bedell Smith, General Walter, 17

Belgium, 11

Berlin, 122

Bernhard, Prince, 17

Bevin, Ernest, 16

Bilderbergers, 1, 11, 17, 18-20

birthright, 47

Blackburn v Attorney General (1983), 45, 46, 47

Blair, Tony, 2, 17, 18

Blake, Lord, 144, 147

Bolick, Clint, 112-117

Bonn, 141

Bosnia, 122

British Coal, 129, 131, 135

Brittan, Sir Leon, 20, 23

Brussels, 40, 122, 141, 152

Bundesbank, 116

Bundesrat, 92, 101

bureaucracy, bureaucrats, 1, 60, 63, 70, 97, 101

Bush, George, 24

bye-elections (absence of), 136

Calhoun, John, 113, 114

Callaghan, Lord, 59, 99

Canada, 26-33, 152

CAP (see Common Agricultural Policy)

Carrington, Lord, 17, 18

Casement, Sir Roger, CMG, 11

Catherwood, Sir Fred, 93

CBI, 138, 140

Central Bank, European, 63, 84, 118

Central Bank (Berlin), 119

Chalker, Baroness, 55, 76

Chamber of Status, 85

Christian Democrat Party, 83, 90, 91, 138, 139

chronology (Maastricht Bill),
    143-145
Churchill, Sir Winston, 1, 7, 16,
    58, 65-68, 71, 153
civil unrest, 70
Clarke, Kenneth, 17, 18, 31, 131
Clinton administration, 132
Committee on Institutional
    Affairs, 86
Committees of the Regions,
    122,125
common action, 41
Common Agricultural Policy
    (CAP), 95, 119
common defence, 62, 63, 84,
    94, 117
Common Fisheries Policy, 61
Common Foreign Policy, 94, 102
Common Labour policy, 125
common law, 43, 79, 107
Common Market, 9, 66, 67
Commonwealth, 3, 67
Communist, 5, 66, 102, 130
Compagnons de France/Vichy,
    137
computers, 135
Confederate States, 48
Conservative/conservatism, 2, 4,
    65, 82-85, 88-96, 107, 128
Conservative Central Office, 82,
    90, 91
Conservative Party Conference
    (1992), 128
Constitution of the European
    Union, 86
Constitution of the USA,
    107-117
Constitution, passim
constitutional crisis, 55
consumer protection, 84
Convergence (economic), 77

Co-prosperity zone, 127
Coronation Oaths Act, 1953, 3,
    12, 13, 37, 46, 54, 55
corporatism, 151, 152
Costa v ENEL (1964), 14, 15,
    117
Cripps, Sir Stafford, 16
Croatia, 122
cross border crime, 84
Crown Counsel, 81
Crown Prerogative, 8, 32, 53,
    128
Crown Prosecution Service, 8,
    10, 52, 79
Culture, Mnistry of, 121
Cumming-Bruce, Lord Justice,
    45
Customs Union, 123

Danish Central Bank, 76, 77
Danish referenda, 64, 143
Declaration of nationality, 49
Defence of the Realm Act
    (DORA), 1914, 15
De Gaulle, General, 59, 97
Delors, Jacques, 63, 124, 126,
    129, 137
democracy, *passim*
democratic deficit, 100, 102,
    105, 106
Denmark, 10, 16, 59, 75-78, 86,
    99, 110, 139, 143
Denning, Lord, 13
Deutschmark, 10
direct elections, 97, 99
directives, 40
Director of Public Prosecutions,
    11
domestic fuel, 74
Donovan, William, 16
Dulles, Allen, 16

Dykes, Hugh, 129

EC/EEC, 8, 72
Economic and Monetary Union
    (EMU), 84
Edinburgh summit, 61, 114
education, 84
Edwina (Mrs. Piers Dixon), 66
energy, 84, 115
English System, the, 120, 124,
    127
English world economy, 123
Enlightcrunent, 107
Environment policy, 85
EPP Manifesto, 82-85, 88-96
Equal Pay Act (1970), 45
Eringer, Robert (author), 17
Eurocrats, 87
Euro-fascists, 5, 48, 65, 126-131
Eurofederalists, 36, 98, 118
Europabank, 119, 125
*Europaische
    Wirtschaftsgemeinschaft*, 119
European Assembly, 99
European Citizenship, 2, 3, 38,
    54, 62, 80, 102, 106
European Coal and Steel
    Community, 15, 123, 134
European Commission, *passim*
European Communities Act,
    1972, 13, 14, 40
European Communities
    (Amendments) Act, 1993, 7,
    10, 51, 53, 81, 143-145
European Community, *passim*
European Constitution (draft),
    86, 87
European Council of Ministers,
    38, 63, 87, 95, 100, 101,
    120, 129

European Court of Human
    Rights, 12, 113
European Court of Justice, 2, 3,
    4, 13, 22, 23, 33, 36, 37, 38,
    39, 45, 54, 55, 56, 61, 62,
    63, 73, 85, 92, 99, 100, 101,
    108, 111, 112, 136
European Currency system, 119,
    121, 125
European Economic Area, 120
European flag, 141
European Parliament Building
    (cost of), 87
European Parliamentary
    Elections Act, 1978, 50, 53
European People's Party (see
    EPP)
European Regional Policy, 122,
    125
European Space, 121, 125
European Union, 2, 35, 37, 38,
    39, 62, 67, 118, 145
European Works Council, 125
'Ever closer union', 62
Exchange Rate Mechanism
    (ERM), 93, 96, 104, 120,
    125, 140

Falkland Islands, 17
Farben, I. G., 118
fascism, 11, 30, 130, 134, 135,
    138, 150, 152
fate *(Schicksal)*, 123
federal, federalism, 82, 88-96,
    101, 102
Federal Constitutional Court
    (German), 4, 15, 35, 75-78,
    98, 145
Ferrers, Earl, 55
Fianna Fail, 91
Final Act, European, 44, 49

Finance Bill (1994), 114
Financial Times, 76
fishing, 2, 3, 149
flag, 42, 141
Flynn, Padraig, 138
Foreign Office (FCO), 39, 56
foreign policy (see common
  foreign policy)
founding fathers, 79, 107
France, 9, 10, 110, 114, 123,
  129, 133, 135
Franco-German, 98
Franco-German armed force, 48
Frankfurt (am Main), 118, 140
Free men, 48
French Constitutional Court, 99
Funk, Walther, Dr., 119, 121
Garel Jones, Tristan, MP, 129
GATT, 24-33, 114, 120, 128
Gauleiter, 6, 120
Gaullists, 91, 99
General Elections, 54, 55, 56
German Constitutional Court
  (see Federal Constitutional
  Court)
German Empire, 123
German National Foundation,
  140
German nationalism, 139
German poets, 123
Germany, 1, 5, 7, 8, 9, 10, 11,
  13, 35, 65, 67, 120, 123,
  129, 130, 132-142
Gilbert, Martin, 65, 66
Giscard d'Estaing, 140
Gorman, Teresa, MP, 125
government by consent, 69
Greece, 137
guest workers, 119

Halsbury's Laws of England, 11

Hamburg, Radio, 12
Hansard, 34
Hansard Society, 37
Harington, Sir John (see title
  page)
health and safety regulations,
  115
Heath, Sir Edward, MP, 7, 12,
  90, 129
Heathrow, 120
Henley, Lord, 77
Henry IV, King, 11
Herald Tribune, 132
Herman, Fernand, MEP, 86
Hexham, Northumberland, 43
Hexham Magistrates Court, 52
Hickenlooper, Senator, 132
Hitler, Adolf, 7, 29, 118-125,
  126, 131, 135
Hitler's Europe (see Today's
  Europe), 125
Home, Lord, 12
Hong Kong, 39
House of Lords, 4, 23, 55,
  57-64, 69, 76, 146-148
Howe, Geoffrey (Lord), 68, 111,
  135, 137
Hunke, Professor, 120, 121, 122
Hurd, Rt. Hon. Douglas, 3, 31,
  32, 36-42, 43-49, 80, 81,
  111, 131, 144

immigration, 39, 84
implied repeal, 31
India, 151
indirect taxation, 72
initiate legislation, 100
Intergovernmental Conference
  (IGC), 98
internal market (see Single
  Market)

interparliamentary co-operation, 106
Iraq, arms to, 79
Ireland, 10, 122
iron curtain, 66
Italy, 114, 119, 129, 130, 133-139

Jackson, Caroline, MEP, 94
Jay, Peter, 17
Jenkins of Hillhead, Lord, 58
Johnson, Boris, 56
Joyce, William, 11, 12
Judicial Committee Act (1833), 81
Judiciary, 62, 70, 80

Karlsruhe, 75, 106, 145
Khasbulatov, Ruslan, 102
Kinnock, Neil, 20-23
Kohl, Helmut (Chancellor), 116, 122, 123, 133, 138, 140
Kyle, David, 52

Labour, 2, 4, 5, 15, 16, 91, 143, 144
Laker Airways, case, 52
Lamont, Norman, 73
Latin America, 151
Leasehold Reform, 111
Lebensraum, 120, 121, 125
Lerwick, Shetland Is., 80, 81
Liberal Democrats, 2, 143, 144
Lincoln, Abraham, President, 35, 48, 113
local elections (see also municipal), 54
Lord Advocate, 10, 81
Lord Chancellor, 80
Luns, Dr. Joseph, 98

Luxembourg Compromise, 45, 59, 60
Lyell, Sir Nicholas, 80

Maastricht Bill (European Communities (Amendment) Act, 1993), 143-145
Maastricht Treaty, passim
  Article 8   22, 23, 44, 46, 49, 62
  Article 8a   39, 44
  Article 8b   44, 45
  Article 99   73
  Article 100c 39
  Article 137a 101
  Article 171 46
  Article 192 44, 46, 49, 80
  Article F   61, 76
  Article J1   41
  Article Q   47
  Article R   15, 75, 77
Macao, 39
McCarthys v Smith (1979), 45
MacDonald, Ramsay, 16
McGhee, George, 17
Macmillan, Harold, 67
Mc Whirter v Attorney General (1972), 13
McWhirter, Norris, 23, 43, 52, 55, 80, 145, 153
Madison, James, 109
Madrid, 132
Major, John, 2, 10, 24, 31, 32, 37, 83, 84, 95, 116, 131
'M Case', 52
Magna Carta, 40, 48
majority voting, 49, 55
maternity benefits, 37, 130
Maude, Rt. Hon. Francis, 44-49, 80
Megarry, Sir Robert, 45, 46, 47

MEP's, 70, 82, 87, 88-106
MEP'S, cost of, 102, 103
mercantilism, 127
Messina, 99
Mexico, 26-33, 152
milk production, 134
Monnet, Jean, 15
Morel, E. D., MP, 15, 16
Morley, Felix, 111
Moseley, Sir Oswald, 11

NAFTA, 24-33
National Front, 130
nationist, 141
NATO, 41, 66, 134
Nelson, Admiral, 68, 153
Nichols v Nichols (1576), 12
Ninth Amendment, 112
Nobel Peace Prize, 16

Old Bailey, 11, 12
Omaha Beach (Normandy), 152

passports, 2, 12, 38, 39
Penders, Jean, 91
pensions, 2
Peru, 11
Polish border, 122
Portugal, 10, 39
Powell, Enoch, 97
Prerogative, 8, 32, 53, 128
Privy Counsellors, prelim.,
  21-23, 42
procrustean, 119
Procurator Fiscal, 79, 81
protectionism, 127
Prout, Sir Christopher, 89
public health, 84

Qualified Majority Voting
  (QMV), 60, 84

Queen Elizabeth I, 12
Queen, Her Majesty The, 2, 3,
  5, 11, 12, 13, 21-23, 33, 34,
  37, 41, 46, 55, 70, 80, 141
Quisling, V. (CBE), 4
quota hopping, 61

ratchet, the, 72
ratification, 53, 58, 75-78, 145
Reagan, Ronald, 24
Rees Mogg, Lord, 10, 81, 128,
  145, 148
referendum, 2, 5, 59, 69, 98,
  110, 111, 143
refugees, 84
regional committees, 120
Reichmark, 119
Reithinger, Dr., 118
research and development, 84
residential rights, 40, 44, 49, 149
resources, biological, 121
resources, human, 121
Retinger, Dr. Joseph, 15, 16, 17
retrospective law, 128
reunification (of Germany), 133
Richtofen, von, Baron, 7, 141
Rippon, Lord (of Hexham), 12
Rockefeller, David, 17, 18
Roll of Honour, Peers, 146-148
Rome, Treaty of, 9, 59, 60, 64,
  72, 73, 74, 77, 80, 134
Roosevelt, F. D., 115
royal assent, 144
RPR (France), 91
rule of law, 5, 59, 136
Rusk, Dean, 17
*R v Secretary of State for
  Foreign and Commonwealth
  Affairs (ex parte* Rees
  Mogg), 81, 145

R v Thistlewood (1820), 45, 46, 47, 49

sanctions, 85
Sandhurst, Royal Military Academy, 152
Schmidt, Helmut, 140
Scotland, 5, 49, 50, 121, 122
Scottish Parliament, 51
SDP (German Social Democratic Party), 140
seat belts, 130, 131
secession, 35, 47, 49
secrecy (see Bilderbergers), 51
Section 301, 27
Seitz, Raymond, 152, 153
self-governance, 69, 80, 97, 131
separation of powers, 136
Settlement, Act of (1700), 12, 36, 45, 46, 47
Sikorski, General, 16
silk (from China), 135
Simmons, Richard, MEP, 94
single currency, 63, 84
single currency (abolition of Pound), 138
Single European Act, 1986, 30, 40, 59, 64, 84, 133
single market, 9, 63, 151
slavery, 35, 48
Smith, Adam, 153
Social Chapter, 5, 63, 85, 90, 115, 120, 131, 143, 144
social policy, 84, 85, 94
sovereignty, 2, 5, 8, 27, 62, 70, 72, 97, 139
Soviet Union, 41, 67, 104, 120, 150, 151
Spaak, Paul-Henri, 98
Spain, 114, 135
Spanish fishing vessels, 61

Speaker (House of Commons), 144
Stalin, Josef, 29
statism, 124, 127, 129
Statute Law Repeals Act, 40, 48
Statute of Proclamations, 53
steel subsidies, 114, 129, 131, 135
Stevens, John, MEP, 93

Stoddart of Swindon, Lord, 54, 55, 148
Story, Christopher, 119
Strasbourg (see European Parliament)
Strasbourg recommendations, 66
Stuttgart, 132
subsidiarity, 36, 60, 61, 70, 84, 85, 93, 112, 116
Sunday Telegraph, 56
suzerainty, 38, 44
Sweden, 110

tax, 38, 46, 49, 72-78, 83, 89, 90
taxation, 130, 142
Taylor, A. J. P., 149
teleconununications, 84
Tenth Amendment (USA), 112, 116
terrorism, 84
Tetens, T. H., 132
Thatcher, Lady, 24, 36, 57, 59-64, 148
The Times, 89
Third Reich, 16, 120
Thompson, Dorothy, 132
Today's Europe (see Hitler's Europe), 125
Tonypandy, Viscount, 57-59, 147
Tory Reform Group, 128
tourism, 84

trade unions, 37, 138
trading deficit, 58
Tralee, Ireland, 11
transport, 84
treason, 13, 43-52, 79, 80
Treason Act, 1795, 43, 44, 47, 49
Treaty of Accession, 13, 14
Treaty of Rome, 9, 13, 22
Treaty on European Union, 44, 48
Turks, 119

UFO's, 102
Ulster, 122
unanimity, 59, 84, 85
Union Jack, 141
Union of Democratic Control, 15, 16
Union with Scotland Act (1707) (see Act of Union), 49, 50, 51
United States of Europe, 67, 89, 122
Uruguay Round, 31
US Congress, 29, 31, 33
US Foreign Affairs Committee, 132
US sovereignty, 32
US Supreme Court, 112, 115, 116
USA, 1, 67, 79, 107, 150, 152
USSR (see Soviet Union)

vassal state, 142
VAT (Value Added Tax), 39, 72, 73, 108, 114
Vauxhall Estates v Liverpool Corporation (1932), 47
Vichy, 134, 137
visa, 39, 40
voting rights, 40, 44, 45, 49, 54, 55

Waigel, Theo, 140
Wales, 5, 122
war, 5, 142
war dead, 48, 69
Wehrmacht, 16
Wellington, Duke of, 68, 111, 153
Westminster Parliament, 36, 51, 55, 63, 64, 70, 122
workers, part-time, 130
workers rights, 37
working hours, 37, 130
World Trade Organization (WTO), 25-33
xenophobia, 104

Your Country, Your Democracy, 151

Yugoslavia, 104, 119, 150

zero rating, 73

Zyklon B gas, 118

Books by Rodney Atkinson

REAL INTEREST (£3.00)
An Alternative to the ERM

"Rodney Atkinson's Real Interest proposal deserves very serious consideration."   Professor Patrick Minford

YOUR COUNTRY YOUR DEMOCRACY (£3.50)
The Threat from the "European" Community

CONSERVATISM IN DANGER (£3.50)
Six Pillars of Conservatism Undermined

"If the Government wants to know what needs to be done Ministers should read Rodney Atkinson's *Conservatism in Danger*"
                     Professor Norman Stone, *Sunday Times*

THE FAILURE OF THE STATE (£4.00)
The Democratic Costs of Government

"Atkinson's latest box of intellectual fireworks"
                     Lord Harris of High Cross
"Closely and cleverly reasoned"   Matthew Parris of *The Times*
"As acute, witty and well documented as ever"   *Encounter*
"A devastating historical analysis of the costs and effects of Regional policy."   *London Evening Standard*

THE EMANCIPATED SOCIETY (£7.50)
State Authority and Individual Freedom

"A powerful argument"   Dr. John Gray, Oxford
"Brilliant"   Professor Norman Barry, Buckingham
"A unique and refreshing defence of liberty"
                     Laissez Faire Books, New York

GOVERNMENT AGAINST THE PEOPLE (£5.00)

"Excellent, fascinating"   Nobel Laureate Milton Friedman
"Excellent, devastating"   George Gilder
"Excessive Government expertly diagnosed"
                     Professor Norman Barry

UK post add 10%. Overseas post add 20%. Cheques to:
Compuprint Publishing, 1 Sands Road, Swalwell,
Newcastle upon Tyne NE16 3DJ.

Other Books on Europe

RESISTING LEVIATHAN - THE CASE AGAINST A EUROPEAN STATE (£3.99)
Philip Van der Elst

IDEALISM WITHOUT ILLUSIONS - A FOREIGN POLICY FOR FREEDOM (£3.00)
Philip Van der Elst

THE TRUTH ABOUT A FEDERAL EUROPE (£0.20 each - minimum order 5 copies)
The Freedom Association

CONSTITUTION OF THE EUROPEAN UNION (£1.80)
Campaign Against Euro Federalism

All available from The Freedom Association,
35 Westminster Bridge Road, London SE1 7JB.